DIET FOR A S
A dietary programme f
and healthily in an o
and an over-populated world.

Also by Patrick Rivers
LIVING BETTER ON LESS (Turnstone Press)
LIVING ON A LITTLE LAND (Turnstone Press)
POLITICS BY PRESSURE
THE RESTLESS GENERATION
THE SURVIVALISTS

DIET FOR A SMALL ISLAND

by

Patrick and Shirley Rivers

TURNSTONE PRESS LIMITED
Wellingborough, Northamptonshire

First published 1981

© PATRICK AND SHIRLEY RIVERS 1981

This book is sold subject to the condition that it shall not, by way of trade or otherwise, be lent, re-sold, hired out, or otherwise circulated without the publisher's prior consent in any form of binding or cover than that in which it is published and without a similar condition including this condition being imposed on the subsequent purchaser.

British Library Cataloguing in Publication Data

Rivers, Patrick
　Diet for a small island.
　1. Cookery
　2. Cookery (Natural foods)
　I. Title
　II. Rivers, Shirley
　641.5'52　　TX652

ISBN 0-85500-137-2

Photoset by Ad' House, Earls Barton, Northamptonshire.
Printed in Great Britain by Nene Litho, Earls Barton,
and bound by Weatherby Woolnough, Wellingborough,
Northamptonshire.

CONTENTS

	Page
Preface	7
Part One	
Chapter	
1. Why This Book	9
2. Arguments for Change	19
3. Towards a More Self-sufficient Britain	47
Part Two	
4. Steps to Creativity	65
5. Soups and Salads	77
6. Mainly Main Dishes	109
7. Desserts, Puddings and Cakes	193
8. Variety in Bread	217
9. This and That	231
Ideas for Action	249
Further Reading	251
Recipe Index	253

To the impoverished millions, that we may
the less condone their hunger.

PREFACE

This is more than a recipe book, though indeed it does have excellent recipes. It is a book about how we can survive in Britain in the imminent future – in perhaps the most vulnerable over-populated island in the world. It urges us to make modest changes to the way we eat so that we can eat more of what we grow in Britain. Essentially it is for people living in cities and towns, and intending to stay where they are, though anyone aiming for much vaunted 'self-sufficiency' will also find it valuable.

There are books about nutrition, health, politics, farming, gardening, ecology, world poverty and hunger. These appeal chiefly to the mind. There is also an indigestible feast of recipe books appealing to the stomach. *Diet For A Small Island* instead offers a 'wholistic' approach – to mind, body and spirit. It looks at all subjects in the first group, comes up with some recommendations, and then offers enough recipes to show how you can put them into practice.

It is written for men and women, but we are sure to be branded sexist by some, simply because we dare to suggest that the kitchen is the most important room in the house. We urge people to spend more time there rather than less, because they *become what they eat*. We say there is a hidden price tag to convenience foods which far outweighs savings in time and money – save today, pay later. We argue that we are not sexist at all because we are asking people to *think* about what they cook and eat. We credit cooks with having minds and consciences, and urge them to ask about what is in our food, what does the growing of it do to the one world we all share, and what does the eating of it do to ourselves, especially our children. We offer answers to these questions, based on a good deal of study, and the answers are frankly disturbing. Nevertheless, out of this examination hope emerges – not blind optimism that *all* the world's problems will be solved, but informed optimism on some crucial aspects about this island's food and health prospects.

1
WHY THIS BOOK

About ten years ago we began asking questions about our food: whether it tasted good, was it doing us good, what was in it, how was it grown and where did it come from. We looked more closely at the food shops, especially at what they sold in packets, and over a period of time our uneasinesss grew into a firm conviction that much of the food on offer was a ghastly mistake, for which people were paying a high price – and not just in money. Put simply, we found we should not be eating that kind of stuff. Instead, we and others should be eating more food which comes fresh from our own gardens and allotments, more produce *direct* from Britain's farms, less through food processing factories, and less from distant places.

We researched and asked more questions and learned that most of us in Britain are suffering from *malnutrition* – not under-nutrition, but over-nutrition – from a diet that is all wrong for the mid-twentieth century. Either we have drifted into it or we are being 'programmed' to eat this way to suit the profitability of the food industry ... or both; but, whatever the cause, the way we eat is patently extravagant, wasteful, unbalanced and potentially dangerous!

Then came the crucial discovery which jolted our consciousness. If we both went some way to putting our diet right – and enough other people did the same – not only would we all be better off in health, pocket and enjoyment, but Britain as a nation need no longer be dependent on others for nearly half her food – in a world facing overall food shortage.

In other words, *the diet best for the people of Britain is the one Britain herself is best able to grow.*

As our modest changes became progressively more cohesive, they acquired a name – The Small Island Diet – which seemed appropriate and soon stuck. One by one its benefits revealed themselves. We found to our surprise that the diet was not plain or stodgy, but full of variety all year round. It was so fresh, with colour and texture – the way food used to taste, or even better. We expected our food bills to rise, but they did not – if anything they shrank.

As we progressively changed our eating habits, we began to feel better for doing so, and some time spent understanding nutrition soon showed why. Then, no less salient, we learned that we were storing up fewer health risks for ourselves in later years.

Changes we made, but they were not faddish. The Small Island Diet cost us no friends. On the contrary, as we were led to stimulatingly fresh interests and wider concerns, countless new friends entered our lives – at an age when most people become set in their ways. We had taken the first steps on a journey of discovery.

The Malnutrition of Affluence

Most of us who live in the 'Rich North' of the world – in industrial countries like Britain – eat far more than we need for an age when machines do so much of the work. The result is that nearly half the people in Britain are overweight and a fifth are obese – 20 per cent heavier than the recognized average weight for average height. The more obese you are, the shorter your expectation of life, as Figure 1 shows only too clearly. For the sedentary sort of lives that most of us lead, we eat too much fat and oil and highly refined foods, especially sugar and white bread. Although one in five of us shows the effects of doing so all too plainly – as ugly fat – nearly all of us pay for the over-indulgence sooner or later with a miscellany of problems, from varicose veins to fatal heart disease. Most of the rest of the world's people, in the 'Poor South', suffer the malnutrition of poverty – under-nutrition – but ironically we all share the same chief consequences: less enjoyment of life, more disease and an earlier death.

In Britain we eat a third more protein than dieticians recommend – far more than our bodies need. Once upon a

Figure 1 The Fatter You Are, the Shorter Your Life

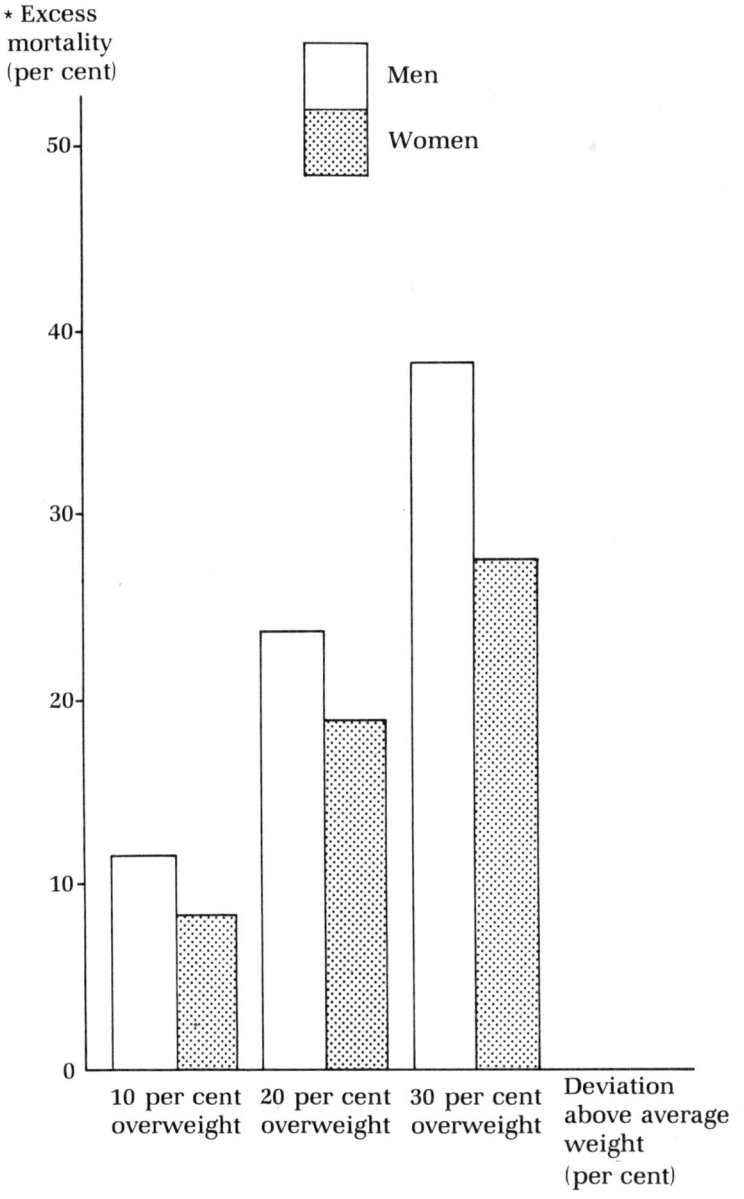

* Excess mortality (per cent)

Men
Women

Deviation above average weight (per cent)	Men	Women
10 per cent overweight	~11	~8
20 per cent overweight	~24	~19
30 per cent overweight	~38	~27

*Compared with all persons insured as standard risks

time it was thought that active people required extra meat, fish, milk, cheese and eggs, but now we know this to be a fallacy. In fact nearly all of us eat too much of these protein-rich foods, and so, enjoyable though we find them, if we are at all budget-conscious, we are simply letting hard-earned money go down the drain, with the dishwater. Also, since most of these foods contain unseen fat, they contribute to the first problem.

We do not eat nearly enough fresh vegetables and fruit. Let's face it: for most people meat comes first. A meal without it wouldn't be a meal. In our research we explored why the tired old joke of 'chips and frozen peas with everything' is still a reality; television commercials apart, it is because they are quick and easy and you know what you are in for. Now Britain grows an amazing variety of other vegetables, but too many of them are ignored because, unless you know how to cook them to perfection, they have a nasty habit of finishing up something of a soggy mess. And then it's back to chips and peas!

If you buy vegetables rather than grow them yourself, however, the let-down when they're cooked isn't all your fault. In later pages we shall explain just why their polythene-wrapped seductiveness in the shops so often degenerates to bland sogginess on your plate – just as we shall offer advice on perfection cooking. More significantly we shall make the outrageous suggestion that in planning a meal you think first of all about the vegetables and which one of umpteen tempting ways you can use to combine and cook them – *before* thinking about the meat, instead of last! Now this should be a help, not only because meat is your most expensive item, but because you have only four sorts of common farm livestock to choose from, whereas there are dozens of different vegetables. Haven't you ever wished someone would invent some new farm animals?

Most of us do not eat enough roughage, and because of this we risk contracting a few more diseases, including cancer. Yet, we would get all our necessary roughage without paying through the nose for patent bran foods if only we ate wholemeal bread rather than 'cottonwool' wrapped white, along with the fresh vegetables and fruit we neglect. But we would also do well to go easy on the pretty packages of over-refined, processed and 'convenience' foods which dominate the supermarket shelves and earn for themselves the nickname 'junk food'. What they lack in roughage they make up in chemical additives: artificial colouring agents, preservatives, stabilizers, emulsifiers, bulking agents, and even artificial flavourings. The food industry has not introduced these chemicals to nourish us, but to persuade us to buy, and to help it market its wares more profitably. Anyone on a Diet of Affluent Malnutrition is likely to eat up to three pounds of them a year – which equals about twelve aspirin-sized tablets a day. A dangerous habit as you'll presently see.

Successive food and health ministries have shown little or no concern over the nation's 'industrial' diet. On the contrary, the Ministry of Agriculture, Food and Fisheries puts up a spirited defence of modern food technology and the industrial colossus it has spawned. If, as they imply, Britons eat healthily, then what is the nation's 'track record' on health? The more sugar we eat, the more prevalent is tooth decay – now costing the country well over £300 million a year. As a nation we are 20 per cent overweight and correspondingly prone to coronary heart disease – coronary thrombosis, unknown to nineteenth-century physicians, now kills some 100,000 people a year. The death rate from cancer is still rising and at least one form of it is associated with our over-refined diet. Doctors write more than 50 million prescriptions in a year for sleeping pills, tranquillizers, anti-depressants and stimulants; while food additives have now been shown to cause mental disorders. We spend over £8,000 million a year on the National Health Service, yet it can barely cope, and private health care has become a rapidly growing business. Social indicators of ill-health are almost limitless. The close relationship between diet and health is firmly established. And the malnutrition of affluence persists.

Food for Profit
Most of us know next to nothing about nutrition. Price, packaging, advertising, habit, fashion, recommendation, impulse ... all these play a part in our choice of food. Nutrition is too often at the bottom of the list. The food industry claims that it responds to people's demands. In our researches we found the reverse to be true. As corner

shops close down in the face of supermarket competition, as small firms succumb to take-overs, and 'big names' spend millions on advertising their brands, while most fresh food is unadvertised, true choice – as compared with spurious choice between almost identical brands – virtually disappears. Under such a barrage, not surprisingly, shoppers find themselves 'programmed to buy junk'.

The power behind the food industry's barrage is formidable. A mere thirty firms now control over half Britain's food manufacturing industry, and just fifty firms control over half the market in distribution. On the land the same trend exists. Family farming as a way of life has given way to 'agribusiness' – huge farms, inexorably linked with the petrochemical companies and the banks, with balance sheets as their guides. The criterion throughout is 'food for profit, not for people'. Nature takes a back seat. In the attendant razzamatazz of marketing gimickry and technological tinkering with chemical additives, her miraculous offerings are prostituted to the status of just another industrial commodity. Farmers produce the contaminated raw materials. Successive governments endorse the trend. The media, through advertising revenue, profit by it. Meanwhile we, the consumers, have been turned into 'junk food junkies' and the huge companies dominating the food industry are 'the pushers'.

Yet, as Richard Mackarness – doctor, psychiatrist and author – has aptly pointed out, food is man's most intimate contact, far more intimate than copulation. Absorbed directly into the bloodstream and carried into every cell in the body, food – along with its modern contaminants – enters and effects even that most vital organ, the brain. These contaminants do not exist in nature: they are the creation of the food industry. They are such a recent innovation that there has not yet been time for extensive study of their mental and physical effects on man. However, most of the evidence beginning to come in suggests that their effects may be harmful, he warns.

It is not difficult to identify one principal reason for the popularity of the convenience foods which are the chief offenders: it is the twentieth century mania for *time-saving* – the compulsion to get out of the kitchen quickly at all costs! The costs, however, may turn out to be measured, not in pence-per-packet, but in terms more horrifying than we dare contemplate. The long-term, poisonous, carcinogenic effects of their chemical additives and chemicals may resemble time bombs implanted in our body tissues, slowly accumulating toxins until triggered to explode at unpredictable intervals.

Yet if question marks hang over their future toxicity, there is no doubt about at least one present concern: research has already shown that, in two out of every three people, they cause allergies, ranging from minor skin rashes to conditions conducive to chronic illness and depression. We believe that their packaging should be labelled: 'Warning. Contents may seriously damage your health.'

Importing Trouble

The Small Island Diet proposes that we should eat food grown close to home rather than far away. It is sheer nonsense to transport vegetables daily from London to Cardiff when they grow splendidly nearby. There is a kind of motorway madness in juggernauts loaded with identical processed foods constantly passing each other in opposite directions. Little wonder that, for every pound spent on food production as it leaves the farm, a further £2 is spent on processing and distribution. This is just one reason why we advocate fresh, local food: not only because it is generally better, but because it is – or obviously should be – less costly.

Clearly enormous savings could be made on the home front, but they are small fry compared with the possibilites in international trading. If enough people in Britain changed to The Small Island Diet, the nation's annual food import bill could shrink from over £6,000 million to a few million. This is not just one more dry statistic but an economic fact of life which could improve the well-being of every family in the land.

Until we began asking questions, we had shared with everyone else the complacent assumption that food would flow to our shores for ever more. Our complacency soon evaporated. Here is the very different picture we unearthed:

- Each year there is less land in the world to grow food for its 4,300 million people. Already there is barely one acre for each person. Within 20 years this is expected to halve, for soil is eroding, deserts are advancing – and there will be nearly 2,000 million more people to feed.

- In the Poor South, where 3,200 million live, some 400 million are desperately hungry most of the time – half of them children. Yet this is where much of our food comes from, and countries there are unlikely to continue feeding us *and our farm animals* while their own people become hungrier. Any food they spare will cost more as it becomes scarcer.

- For a time Britain may be able to pay for food imports, in part by exporting North Sea oil, but as this runs out she will have to rely more on revenue from industrial exports. Her indifferent industrial performance will face increasing competition abroad as production rises in her traditional markets.

- Wars, droughts and famines are likely to multiply in a world of mounting social and environmental crises. Britain will be vulnerable to resultant interruptions in food supplies.

- Memberhip of the European Economic Community will offer slender protection from worldwide trends.

In short, any nation which fails to grow most of its own food, when it is perfectly able to, puts itself in a dangerously dependent position; and that is simply another way of saying that every family in Britain is endangered.

Britain has been importing about half her food for so long that anyone challenging the practice is sure to meet stiff opposition. One familiar argument is that our home output is near its limit, another that the resultant diet would be dull and nutritionally lacking, another that the developing countries of the Poor South would suffer. In the following pages we present strong evidence to the contrary and offer the hopeful conclusion that Britain's future food supplies need not be at risk. If her people were to change to The Small Island Diet, and Officialdom would provide support with an appropriate National Food Policy to help farmers make the transition, Britain's fertile land could meet most of her needs.

Let us make one point clear right away. This does not imply *total* self-sufficiency. That would be a nonsense. We all have to distinguish between, on the one hand, the *dependency* of importing daily staple foods – such as cereals for feeding ourselves and our animals, and indeed meat itself; and, on the other hand, the *neutrality* of irregularly importing the minor essentials and the major morale boosters which we cannot grow – such as spices, oils and exotic fruits.

A huge saving in the cost of food imports would not be the only financial benefit to Britain. Because the Small Island Diet is a healthier way to eat, we would each be practising *preventative* medicine. In contrast, The Diet of Affluent Malnutrition encourages sickness, and so incurs cost to both the nation, and to its people as individuals, when they foot the bills for *curative* medicine. The National Health Service would then assume a role more appropriate to its name, and cost a good deal less.

The Small Island Diet sets out to restore food to its deserved status – as a bringer of health, not a destroyer; as a means to foster each nation's self-reliance, rather than debilitating dependence. In short: to see food for people, not for profit. In the next chapter we show how simple alternatives can restore to eating the enjoyment which nourishes, while keeping this experience within the means of everyone.

2
ARGUMENTS FOR CHANGE

Traditional British food was once among the best in the world. Today our palates have become so dulled by badly grown food, which is then over-processed and insensitively cooked, that we in Britain apathetically accept a travesty of British food which other countries see as a bad joke.

The last chapter identified the chief reasons for this sad deterioration; now we go more deeply into what is wrong and how it may be put right. In advocating The Small Island Diet we are not urging you to switch from meat and two veg to mung beans and brown rice overnight. Nor is what we propose the final answer, either to the problems of your own well-being or Britain's. All that we are suggesting is that you eat rather less and a little differently. Here, one by one, are the changes we recommend, and the reasons why.

You don't need to be a nutritionist to know when you are over-eating. The commonest and most obvious symptom is overweight. Other signs are: lassitude and a feeling of fullness after meals; indigestion; eating when you are not hungry and having second helpings when you are satisfied. In plain words – greed! Commonsense and conscience must be your guides. Everyone knows that a person constantly engaged in heavy or physically demanding work needs more to eat than someone who spends most of the time sitting down. If you are in the second group, or your regular exercise is so undemanding that you don't even get out of breath, then clearly you are over-eating if you have a hearty breakfast, a good lunch and evening meal, with a few snacks, tea, coffee and alcoholic drinks in between.

You could do a course on nutrition or read books on it, and we wouldn't say 'no' to either. But we know that most people will shirk nutrition tables and sums, and seek a simpler guide. Let's face it, most of us are capable of knowing when we are eating more than we need.

It is a good idea to have some bathroom scales in the house. Compare what you weigh with what you should weigh, and then check weekly with a view to steadily reducing. Figure 2 shows you what you should weigh in pounds, wearing indoor clothes, according to your height and frame. The recommended weights are those of people over 25 in the United States who have been found to live longest. The closer you can get to the recommended weight, the longer you're likely to live.

The trouble is that over-eating becomes a habit. Stomachs expand according to the amount of food they are accustomed to receiving – however protestingly! If you suspect you are eating more than you need, try eating less for long enough for your stomach to adjust, and see if you feel better. Only a growing child, an adolescent, an adult engaged in heavy physical activity or a pregnant woman needs three good meals a day – though pregnancy and obesity are incompatible. For others, either the big lunch or big evening meal can go – as can the snacks and drinks in between; except, of course, pure water, if you can get it, for most of us drink too little water already. Don't go on a 'crash diet' for that can be dangerous. Instead cut down gradually and follow the suggestions we offer in this book.

We have already touched on the reasons why over-eating is unwise. We shall return to them as we discuss the different kinds of food commonly eaten in excess.

Why the Fuss about Proteins?
There are three chief reasons why we need proteins – the nutrients commonly known to predominate in meat, fish, milk, cheese and eggs, though also plentiful in beans, peas and grains. For a start, one fifth of our weight is proteins: our bones, skin, muscles, tendons, cartilage, hair, nails and blood all abound in them. Children especially need plenty of proteins in their diet in order to grow, but all of us need them to repair wear and tear of our bodies. Then we need certain proteins as hormones and enzymes for our

Figure 2 What You Should Weigh

Height (in shoes) ft in	Small frame lb	Medium frame lb	Large frame lb
Men			
5 2	112-120	118-129	126-141
5 3	115-123	121-133	129-144
5 4	118-126	124-136	132-148
5 5	121-129	127-139	135-152
5 6	124-133	130-143	138-156
5 7	128-137	134-147	142-161
5 8	132-141	138-152	147-166
5 9	136-145	142-156	151-170
5 10	140-150	146-160	155-174
5 11	144-154	150-165	159-179
6 0	148-158	154-170	164-184
6 1	152-162	158-175	168-189
6 2	156-167	162-180	173-194
6 3	160-171	167-185	178-199
6 4	164-175	172-190	182-204
Women			
4 10	92-98	96-107	104-119
4 11	94-101	98-110	106-122
5 0	96-104	101-113	109-125
5 1	99-107	104-116	112-128
5 2	102-110	107-119	115-131
5 3	105-113	110-122	118-134
5 4	108-116	113-126	121-138
5 5	111-119	116-130	125-142
5 6	114-123	120-135	129-146
5 7	118-127	124-139	133-150
5 8	122-131	128-143	137-154
5 9	126-135	132-147	141-158
5 10	130-140	136-151	145-163
5 11	134-144	140-155	149-168
6 0	138-148	144-159	153-173

metabolism – the complex reactions which convert our food to energy and tissue. And we need others to help fight infection.

Proteins are complex substances containing up to 22 amino acids. These acids consist of carbon, oxygen and nitrogen, and sometimes sulphur. Each species of animal and vegetable has its own characteristic proteins – its own key number and proportions of amino acids. Now some foods contain more proteins than others, notably fish, fowl and lean meat. Flesh is richer in proteins than most plants are, and some vegetables and cereals are richer than others. The plants with the most proteins are the legume family, such as beans and peas, which not only absorb nitrogen to make proteins in the way other plants do – from salts in the ground – but also have the unique ability to obtain it from the air. Legumes may be high in the protein league but cereals are not to be spurned as sources of proteins, nor are some non-leguminous vegetables. However, to get worthwhile amounts from them you have to eat larger quantities and absorb other nutrients as well – and you may have enough of these already.

Since the protein characteristic in each species is unique, it is not surprising that the food value to us of each protein varies. The best species are those with a number and proportion of amino acids which most closely resemble our own. On this basis animals, fish and fowl contain a better quality of protein than any cereal or vegetable. However, you can get more benefit from plant protein by eating complementary foods at the same meal, so that the amino acids lacked by one source may be made up by the other. In practice the only combination you need worry about is legumes and cereals. Cereals are short of *lysine*; legumes are rich in it, yet they are low in *methionine* which is adequate in cereals. This means that if you eat wholemeal bread with your peas or beans, for example, you will get more benefit – if indeed more proteins are what you need.

Knowing what proportions of amino acids each of the different protein sources contain would enable you to work out how to get the most from various combinations. If you had chosen to be a vegan – one who eats neither flesh nor eggs nor dairy products – or you were intending to adopt something close to the minimum diet for your basic needs, such calculations might be worth doing. However, on a diet as nutritious and varied as the one we propose, you are most unlikely to go short of proteins, even though we do recommend you to eat less meat, fish, fowl and eggs than most people eat now.

You can do this because nutritionists now know that they had grossly over-estimated our protein requirements. Moreover they used to believe that people doing heavy work needed more proteins than others. Such people don't, however, they simply need more food! We also know that people get more of their proteins from previously unexpected sources – for example, in a typical diet, more from bread alone than from cheese, eggs and fish together.

Throughout this book we intentionally avoid recommending the precise amounts of specific foods you should eat each day or each week, and for at least two good reasons. For one thing, you would have to do calculations for each member of the family in units called 'calories' based on each one's sex, age and life style – and we can't see this happening in the average household. For another, you would have to stick to your findings, serving each individual different weights and proportions of foods. Instead we make broad recommendations and rely on your common sense and consciences to follow them.

Bear in mind that although children are not yet full-size, their often amazing appetites are necessary for growth and activity. They should eat plenty, especially protein-rich foods, though – as we shall discuss later – not too many sweet foods; small people need less food than large people, and therefore women usually less than men; pregnant women somewhat more, though not 'enough for two'; and old people rather less again. Active people need more food than sedentary people, though, as we have said, not extra proteins – and a mother can be among the most active of all.

Those who feel comforted by figures might be helped to know that a meat-eating adult needs about 0.01 oz. of proteins a day for each pound of bodyweight. This means 2.2 oz. (approx. 65 g) for an 11 stone man and 1.8 oz. (approx. 45 g) for a 9 stone woman. Now no food is all proteins – it contains water, fat, starch and fibre in varying degrees.

For example, fish is about 20 per cent proteins and meat about 25 per cent. In theory if this man ate 10 oz. (275 g) of fish or 9 oz. (250 g) of meat he would be getting all his day's protein needs. In practice, however, almost everything else he ate would also contribute: for example just one pint of milk or three eggs would also give him 2.2 oz. (approx. 65 g) of proteins. If nothing else, this shows how unnecessary it is to eat meat every day. With thought and a little time you could well be down to eating meat no more than two or three times a week. Try our suggested meat-extending recipes; serve smaller portions; plan meals round good, properly cooked vegetables, seasoned when appropriate with herbs or spices; serve cheese as a main dish rather than an after-meal-extra; progressively eat fewer eggs and less fish. You should not find the change too painful.

What about the much heralded meat substitutes of flavoured textured plant protein? For those firmly 'hooked' on meat these processed foods may help to ease the transition, but otherwise we do not recommend them. They are an expensive way of eating vegetable proteins which could be eaten as nature intended, rather than through some factory, adding colouring and flavouring but not nutrition. And they are made chiefly from soya beans which are imported.

All right, so you reduce your protein intake closer to the level your body actually requires. What are the benefits?

Proteins are easily the most expensive of all the regularly eaten foods in the average family. If you eat more than your body requires, the way to save most money is to break the meat habit. The average Briton spends a third of his food bill on meat alone, and he is probably already getting all the proteins he needs – and more – from the fish, eggs, cheese and milk not included in that third! You should enjoy better health. Even lean meat is up to one third fat, and fat – as we shall presently see – is a major health hazard when you eat too much of it as most of us do. But that's not all. With the growth of 'agribusiness', livestock farmers regularly use antibiotics to reduce infection and promote growth. Chemical hormones also speed the growth of their livestock, and processors later inject them with chemicals to improve flavour and colour, and to increase water content – especially in frozen chicken. Again, additives to avoid.

Fish were once the safest of foods, but now they too have their 'additives', for the oceans are polluted with DDT, heavy metals and radio-activity, all of which lodge in the fish we eat – the less the better.

Milk, much advertised as a safe, natural food, is sadly not free from suspicion. In fact, it is not a *natural* food for adults at all, and unless they have regularly been fed milk beyond infancy they lack the enzymes needed to digest it. Milk has been shown to be one of the causes of depression and unexplained fatigue, and – more seriously – of ulcerative colitis, a highly distressing and sometimes fatal disease whose victims are often youthful adults. Also it was found in tests that one in five sufferers of migraine, dyspepsia and eczema were cured when they stopped drinking cow's milk. Fortunately, however, when milk has been soured, as in yogurt and cheese-making, many of its harmful effects are neutralized.

More Peace of Mind

On The Small Island Diet you should enjoy a clearer conscience, and for several sound reasons. Much of our imported meat comes from countries where under-nutrition is rife. We import feedstuffs, including high-protein fish-meal, to feed our own livestock for beef, bacon, poultry and eggs. Many of these feedstuffs are grown in countries where people are hungry, but are too poor to buy food at prices paid by our farmers.

By getting more of our proteins direct as grain, rather than indirectly as meat or eggs, we are releasing land to grow food at a time when the amount of agricultural land to support each person in the world is shrinking. This is because it takes at least eight ounces of grain to produce one ounce of animal proteins.

Much of the meat and nearly all the eggs we eat are produced under conditions of factory farming and extreme cruelty. Consider battery hen houses where nearly all Britain's eggs are laid. In a typical one you will find about 3,000 birds, almost immobilized, six to a cage about 1 ft 6 in. square. In stench and gloom they live on processed food for twelve months before slaughter. Under such conditions, unless they are regularly fed antibiotics, fungicides and tranquillizers, they die.

The facts are inescapable, yet ignored daily by a nation of animal lovers, simply so that they can buy their food on the cheap. Is it possible to sit down and *enjoy* veal, bacon, chicken or eggs once we know that to do so is to condone suffering? And do you suppose that such food is good for us?

There are alternatives. We could still eat as much meat and as many eggs as our bodies need; our food bills could even shrink, and farm animals and birds would not suffer. Even if delicious free-range eggs cost up to twice as much as cruelly produced and insipid battery eggs, we could eat half as many. By following the rest of our recommendations we would still all be better fed. Whether the produce is eggs, poultry, veal, pork or bacon, remember that the food from factory 'farms' is cheaper simply because the creatures are treated like machines. If we cannot buy veal, pork, bacon and poultry guaranteed not to come from such places, better to stick to beef, lamb and mutton. At least the animals will have spent most of their lives grazing naturally.

Since, as a nation, we eat too much protein, the chances are that when we've lowered our intake of meat and other high-protein foods we shall still be eating enough of it. If in doubt, we should remember that Britain has an abundance of excellent home-grown produce which contains plenty of proteins, and this can serve as an alternative. The humble potato for example is an unsuspected, rich source.

As you will see from the recipe section, there is a variety of ways for you to enjoy peas and beans all year round – especially delicious when fresh from the garden in summer and, if you like, in warming soups for winter. You will probably be surprised too at the possibilities for cereals – wheat, oats and barley. You should be able to buy good wholemeal bread – not the more common white dyed brown 'with permitted colouring' – if you insist on it and hunt around a little. For the real 'nutty' taste of wholemeal though, there is nothing like your own home-baked – if you have the kind of oven to make home baking economical.

It's all in the mind. Once you recognize that cutting your meat bills to a sensible size is more of a liberation than a deprivation, a whole new world of varied and tasty dishes awaits you.

The Other Energy Crisis

If proteins are the body's building blocks, then carbohydrates, fats and oils are its fuel. They all consist of various arrangements of carbon, hydrogen and oxygen atoms which we 'burn' in chemical reactions to change the energy they hold into energy we can use.

Let's look at carbohydrates first. We eat these chiefly as starch and sugar in cereals, vegetables, sugar cane and fruit, and they form the bulk of the average diet, supplying about half the energy we need. Digesting and absorbing carbohydrates is a fairly simple process of changing them to glucose, which the blood carries round as a readily available source of energy for its various organs. When we eat a meal or snack or have a drink, the body's complex controls remove any excess glucose first to the liver and muscles and later to the body's fat layers, mostly under the skin, where it forms 'energy banks' to be drawn on gradually in lean times. Most of us enjoy an uninterrupted supply of carobohydrates, however, so anything more than a thin layer of fat is totally unnecessary. Too much is not merely ugly, it can be really dangerous, as we shall see.

We use our blood sugar to provide energy all the time even when we are asleep. This is to maintain our involuntary activities of breathing, blood circulation and so on. It usually comes as a surprise when we learn that most of us use more energy for these essentials than for the voluntary activities of working, walking, running and so on. The more physically active we are, the more 'energy' food we need for both kinds of activities. Another common surprise is that brainwork, no matter how active, demands no measurable increase in the intake of 'energy' foods – all of which makes questionable the whole *raison d'être* for expense account lunches!

The study of nutrition is full of surprises, and this itself should be no surprise, since nutrition is such a complicated process. Talking of 'building blocks' and 'energy foods' helps to simplify it, though it does create the risk of oversimplifying. For example if any of us over-indulge in protein we use that as fuel too, but when we do we use only the carbon, hydrogen and oxygen atoms, discarding the expensively acquired nitrogen atoms. This is a wasteful habit, which needlessly inflates our food bills. It is one of the chief reasons why The Small Island Diet advocates eating less protein than most of us have grown used to.

All foods interact to keep the body in balance and in health. Anyone wanting to go further into nutrition can choose from a wealth of books on the subject, some of which you'll find in our list of Further Reading.

Carbohydrates, then, are not merely 'energy' foods. In their natural state they usually contain, among other nutrients, cellulose, more commonly known as roughage or fibre. Even though we cannot absorb cellulose, it is still a nutrient, for it speeds the rate at which food travels through the intestines – neither so fast that we fail to absorb nutrients from other foods, nor so slowly that it dries out to an uncomfortable hardness.

There is evidence to suggest that a lack of roughage is linked with a number of diseases, some fatal. One is the diverticulitis in which the walls of the intestine become so weakened by straining and hard stools that they bulge and become painfully inflamed. Another is varicose veins, for constipated people repeatedly strain when opening their bowels, creating pressure in the abdomen which may affect blood circulation in the legs. Yet another is gallstones – evidence is not conclusive, but convincing enough for anyone, whose diet may be deficient in roughage, to eat more of it. There is so much to be gained and nothing to lose!

Because a diet which lacks fibre is often over-rich, eating too many over-refined foods with no fibre leads to obesity – and disease. One consequence is the diabetes of middle age, for anyone 20 per cent overweight is more than twice as likely to develop it. Middle-age diabetes is on the increase, already four times more prevalent than juvenile diabetes. Coronary heart disease is an even more serious consequence, for over-fat people are similarly bigger targets for this killer disease. Fibre in the diet may help to reduce the level of cholesterol in the blood. Equally serious is cancer of the bowel. Not only may this be brought on by certain bacteria in the bowel which cause carcinogens, but the slow passage of waste, which characterizes a lack of fibre, increases the concentration of these bacteria.

Now it must be stressed that, as so often happens, it is not always possible to prove by tests all the manifest links between cause and effect of disease, but it does seem foolhardy to disregard warnings which deserve to be taken seriously, when the preventative measures can be simple and agreeable.

Figure 3 The Goodness of Whole Wheat

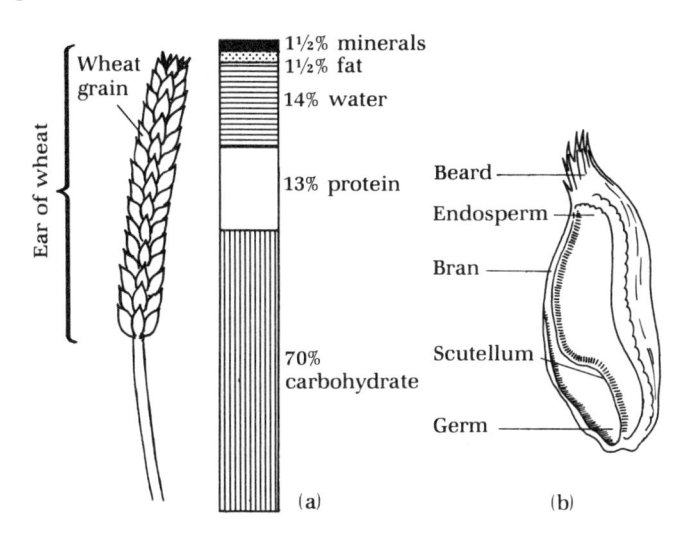

Ear of wheat { Wheat grain

1½% minerals
1½% fat
14% water
13% protein
70% carbohydrate

Beard
Endosperm
Bran
Scutellum
Germ

(a)   (b)

a) What whole wheat contains.
b) Parts of a grain of wheat.

Of course it is easy to become obsessed with the bowel, especially when bad diet forces so many of us to spend far too long under strain in the lavatory – a place where the presence of a bookshelf should be taken as a warning! As a nation of lazy chewers we spend over £5 million a year on laxatives. Yet the *free* roughage in wholemeal flour bread, fresh fruit and vegetables can save this waste, as well as the money spent on expensively advertised bran additives. As you can discover in our recipes, The Small Island Diet, balanced with these foods, is varied and delicious – at least the equal of traditional British food.

Today we are all being 'programmed'. Seventy per cent of what Britain spends on food now goes on the processed variety. What are the over-refined foods which cause us concern? Look along the shelves of any food store and you will see package after colourful package of convenience foods based on white flour – cakes and pudding mixtures, pastas and so on. Look at menus and you will find pies and pasties and pastries predominating. Study shopping bags and four-fifths of the bread is white. The white flour, which is the main ingredient in all these foods has had nearly all the wheat germ and bran removed in the milling process. These valuable nutrients have then been sold separately at a handsome profit. Most of the wheat germ and some of the bran has been put in fancy packages and sold at fancy prices in so-called 'health food' shops; the rest of the bran has been divided between the animal feedstuff business and the booming breakfast cereal business, where it is heavily advertised and colourfully packaged. By now the millers and their friends have made fools of us all!

Now white bread is not only deficient in roughage; it shares with so many other commercially processed foods the potential danger of non-nutritious additives. There are two kinds of additives. One kind is used to improve a food's taste, texture, colour and keeping qualities; the other assists the manufacturing processes. Let's take a quick look at a few of the ones in your daily bread. To bleach it there are *benzoyl peroxide* and *lipoxidase*; to puff up the loaf, the oxidizing agent *potassium bromate*; to make it 'stay fresh longer', *calcium propionate*: to 'soften' it, *mono-* and *di-glycerides*, which are also anti-staling agents and volume boosters; to help processing, the 'free flowing agents *tricalcium phosphate* and *magnesium carbonate*. Among other additives are *chalk, iron* and the B vitamins *niacin, thiamine mononitrate* and *riboflavin*, which are supposed to 'enrich' the bread, but really do little more than replace artificially naturally occurring nutrients removed in the industrial milling to which the wheat is subjected. Predictably there is the all-too-familiar *sugar* too; and for good measure *skim milk powder* and *lard*.

It should be mentioned that besides the usual long-term potential hazards of the chemical additives in general, there is the immediate risk that both these and some of the natural additives may cause distressing allergies – in people allergic to cow's milk for example, who will be unaware they are eating skim milk.

Of course, all food additives are tested to minimize the likelihood that they are carcinogenic – cancer inducing – or otherwise poisonous, but cancers can take years to form and may only do so in association with other agents. These risks just cannot be excluded in relatively short-term laboratory tests.

White flour and white bread, as made commercially today, are no longer natural foods but industrial products, and we, the consumers, pay the costs – many of them unneccesary. Take shipping over long distances as an example. The baking industry aims for a loaf which will keep. This means the addition of water up to the permitted limit, not strictly necessary, but water is cheaper than flour! This means *steaming* rather than baking, which in turn requires a *hard* wheat which Britain cannot normally grow. So we import up to 70 per cent of our bread-making wheat – over half of it from North America. Yet you can bake a superb loaf, white or wholemeal, from all-British flour. People have for centuries!

As authors we would of course be accused of decadent nostalgia if we dwelt on the days when farmers' wheat went straight to the nearest miller and from him to bakers close by, as flour for the splendid loaves they baked for people whose faces they knew. Even people in cities once enjoyed bread derived this way. Today the largely imported raw materials for the 'cottonwool' industrial loaf are hauled long journeys from ports to huge mills and from there to distant, equally huge bread factories before their last long trip to supermarkets. But this is progress ...

The extraordinary way that manufacturers make Britain's bread is dictated primarily by the requirements of the Chorleywood process developed by the Flour Milling and Baking Research Association. It is hardly because people *want* the 'British loaf', for really bread sales have been falling consistently for a generation. Instead it is because, by minimizing labour costs and adding chemicals, manufacturers can turn it out more quickly, cheaply and thus more profitably. All processed foods carry unwarranted transport costs, along with heavy packaging and advertising costs, few of which are justified, and most of which are eliminated or reduced to sensible proportions when food is grown close to where it will be eaten fresh. Long-distance transport, processing and fancy packaging belong to the age of cheap energy, now over. As their costs rise, the case for closely scrutinizing them gains strength.

Sweet Justice
The most refined 'energy' food is sugar. It contains no other nutrients. The higher the country's standard of living, the more of its carbohydrates its people eat in the form of sugar. On average in Britain we eat over 1½ lb (740 g) of cane and beet sugar each week – more than we once used to eat in a whole year. A housewife buys only about half of this a week as straight sugar. The rest comes as 'hidden' sugar, as major ingredients or unsuspected additives to processed and convenience foods, including such unlikely ones as meat stew and baked beans, and in all soft drinks. We also eat appreciable amounts of sugar, or its equivalent, in milk, fruit, vegetables and honey. Whatever their original form, all sugars must enter the bloodstream as glucose, and when the level gets too high our bodies' controls have to remove the excess and either store or excrete it.

Such amounts are not only unnecessary and extravagant, they are unquestionably harmful. To justify such an appetite we would have to be doing the heaviest work imaginable – hewing coal, or cutting sugar cane! Even then, unless we cleaned our teeth after every meal or sweetened drink, we would still suffer from tooth decay – *dental caries*. Sugar is the prime cause because it sticks to the teeth and encourages bacteria which attack them.

Compared with the other potential dangers in over-eating sugar, losing our teeth seems trivial. Once again, the evidence of sugar's links with a number of diseases is not conclusive, but no one has yet proved excess sugar to be safe. Because it increases uric acid in the blood, it may be a cause of gout. We saw how over-refined foods are thought to cause middle-age diabetes; the link with sugar too is understandably strong, for eating too much of it also leads to overweight. For that reason coronary heart disease becomes a greater risk. Still more disturbingly, however, sugar may play an even greater role than fats in the onset of the disease, since it has been shown to increase cholesterol and the ease with which blood clots.

What too few people know or accept is the awkward truth that the healthiest diet of all is one which is completely free of sucrose – that is, cane or beet sugar. The naturally occurring sugars in the other foods we eat, together with a proper intake of carbohydrates and fats, are quite enough to provide all the energy needs of even the most active of us. The sugar addiction from which most of us suffer in varying degrees is yet one more unnecessary item in the food bill of The Diet of Affluent Malnutrition.

How then to cut down on it? The task is not easy, for the habit is drug-like in its persistency, and as yet there is no substitute which can be guaranteed as safe. However, if you change to eating more fresh food, as we suggest, and stop buying processed and convenience foods, at a stroke you will eliminate the 'hidden' sugar which forms up to three-quarters of your intake. Beverages are responsible for much of the remaining consumption, so if you can reduce from, say, two spoonsful in tea and coffee to one, and maybe have one cup instead of two or three, you will be taking another big step. Later you will see how we advise on cooking with less sugar – automatically halving the sugar content in conventional recipes for a start. And if at the end of the day you are still eating too much sugar for a sedentary life style, try stepping up your exercise to match your intake – doctors stress the value of sensible exercise in keeping healthy.

All this is good stuff, but none of us would have to suffer either the withdrawal symptoms of sugar addiction or the consequences of failing to give it up if we had not been introduced to the habit as children. Once early eating habits are formed they become deeply ingrained and the very devil to change. As parents, then, we have a heavy responsibility in protecting our children. Their future is in our hands.

Start young. Avoid any bought baby foods with sugar as an ingredient – far better to make up their foods yourself anyway. Give them no sweetened drinks. Later if they ask for something between meals, first find out why they are hungry, and if it is not because their meals are inadequate, or they are simply bored from inattention, or copying mother, give them a piece of apple or other fruit, a scrubbed carrot or celery, or a little cheese, instead of the usual biscuit or piece of chocolate. They will probably develop a taste for savoury food instead of one for sweetness, if you persist gently but firmly. Sadly, however, many parents abandon hope before even trying, because they fear that their children will be mocked for seeming 'different', or that they will be lured to the school tuck shop anyway. Neither is inevitable. As in so many ways, if parents show loving concern, children will resist alternative influences, and seeming 'different' won't worry them. Instead – as we have both witnessed – the other children are likely to demand that *their* parents provide them with an apple or savoury snack too!

Fats, Oils and Controversy
Fats and oils are fine in moderation. They help to make food palatable; weight for weight they supply twice as much usable fuel as carbohydrates and proteins; and, because they slow digestion, they postpone hunger. Also they supply vitamins. Oil, by the way, is fat which is liquid at room temperature.

Fats do create problems, however. Not all fat is visible, and – not unlike the hidden sugar problem – about half our fat intake is unsuspected. We think of fat only as butter, margarine, cooking fats and oils, and salad oils, and ignore other sources. Yet even lean meat can contain up to 30 per cent fat, bacon 40 per cent, cheese 35 per cent or more; while nuts, oatmeal, poultry and some fish, such as herrings, mackerel, pilchards, salmon, sardines and tuna all contain appreciable amounts of fat or oil. Boiled potatoes contain no fat at all, but chips are one third fat! Milk is also a 'hidden' source, and accounts for no less than 17 per cent of our total fat intake.

Again, like sugar, fat in a diet is an indicator of affluence. As a nation, we get about 40 per cent of our dietary energy from fat; the figure has risen steadily for years and is still doing so, even though a safe level would be 20 to 30 per cent. Why safe? One of the problems with fat is its concentration. You can eat more of it than carbohydrate before feeling full, and because one ounce of fat equals

2.3 oz. (approx. 58 g) of carbohydrate in 'energy' value, you are all the more likely to put on weight, and then – as we have seen – you can expect diabetes, coronary heart disease, problems in pregnancy and a shorter life.

But this is not all: you may well be a candidate for varicose veins and disease of the gall bladder too. And be careful how you move around, for fat people are statistically a good deal more accident-prone!

Now fat is not a simple substance, but exists in three forms: saturated, unsaturated and poly-unsaturated. The first is found in animal products, eggs, ordinary margarine, ice cream, chocolate and coconut; the second in poultry, most nuts and olive oil; and the third in other vegetable oils, including wheat germ, 'special' margarine, fish and walnuts.

Most of the saturated fats in the first group are solid at room temperature whereas the rest are mostly liquid, but by far their most important differences are their links with cholesterol level in the blood. Saturates tend to raise it, unsaturates to be neutral and poly-unsaturates to lower it. About the connection between a high blood cholesterol level and coronary heart disease, controversy is rife, but until medical scientists reach a convincing agreement, it makes sense to eat less fat, especially saturated fats. At present we eat about four times as much of them as we do the others.

Whatever its causes, coronary heart disease – high blood pressure, heart attacks and strokes – is not to be glossed over. In the past twenty-five years the number of people dying from it has doubled, and it now kills one man in three over the age of forty. If you find difficulty in cutting down fats there are at least five other steps that doctors advise you to take: do not overeat generally, avoid stress, take more sensible exercise, don't drink too much alcohol, and don't smoke at all.

Suppose you succeed in breaking your sugar addiction and freeing yourself from fat dependence, and suspect you aren't getting enough energy foods. What can replace them? Once again we turn to locally grown produce: the cereals, vegetables and fruit of Britain. As a balanced food, abundant in energy, wholemeal bread is ideal for all except the unfortunate minority allergic to wheat. For most of us, however, there's nothing to equal a well-baked loaf, made from the wheat of these islands. It needs but a fraction of the jam and butter or margarine that 'cottonwool' wrapped white demands to help it go down.

Vegetables, cooked or in a variety of salads, will satisfy your energy needs without damaging your health, and there are dozens to choose from. The table on pages 68-70 shows you how you can eat vegetables and fruit, either fresh or stored naturally, the whole year round.

Often we feel like urging people to dig up their lawns and flower beds if necessary, simply to enjoy the taste and pride of 'growing your own'. Until you've eaten freshly picked summer vegetables, raw or lightly cooked, alone or with herbs, you have missed one of life's delights. In winter, too, vegetables will satisfy your energy needs, in soups and casseroles, in 'bakes' and other tempting dishes – as the recipes will show. So too will fruit, especially the early gooseberries, strawberries, raspberries and blackcurrants which tell us winter is gone and a long, rich harvest of orchard and garden produce lies ahead.

Will I Lack Minerals and Vitamins?

Anyone motivated to follow The Small Island Diet is likely to ask this question. Chemist shops and health food shops thrive on little bottles of these 'essentials' to nutrition. It isn't hard to see why. On the Diet of Affluent Malnutrition you may lack some of them. Any deficiencies will show up as a feeling of malaise, and children's growth will be affected. The Small Island Diet however is balanced and normally abundant in them. Let's look first at minerals.

About fifteen minerals are known to be essential to health, seven of them are present in our bodies in fairly large amounts, and they are called the *major minerals*, the rest are known as *trace elements*. The most abundant mineral in the body is calcium, 99 per cent of it in bones and teeth. Foods extra rich in the mineral are milk, cheese, watercress and white flour – this due to added chalk. Eggs and green vegetables are also good natural sources, especially cabbage. A lack of calcium – very rare in Britain today – results in rickets. Iron is another major mineral, and more than half the amount in a healthy adult is in the blood. A deficiency results in anaemia. Liver and wholemeal bread are the richest sources, but any meat, potatoes and vegetables contribute. Phosphorus is another major mineral, but a deficiency of it never occurs, even though it is the second most abundant mineral in the body, because it exists in nearly all foods. The other major minerals are potassium, sodium and chlorine. Common salt is sodium chloride. Too little intake may bring on muscular cramps, while – more seriously – a habitually high intake may be associated with high blood pressure. Very young infants are intolerant to high intakes, and so salt should not be added to their diets.

The more important trace elements are cobalt, copper, chromium, fluorine, iodine, manganese and zinc. Deficiencies of any mineral, bar phosphorus, can occur but only in people on exceptionally impoverished or unbalanced diets.

The commonest vitamin deficiency is vitamin C which we all need for healthy tissues. Virtually all of it comes from fruit and vegetables, and if we eat too little of them we put ourselves at risk.

Once vegetables are harvested, their vitamin C content falls hourly, so if they are a few days old when you buy them, or you don't eat them at once, they will deteriorate. 'Instant' mashed potato contains no vitamin C unless it has been added artificially in processing. Really fresh food is invariably preferable to frozen food in taste and texture – in the long run – on a cost basis, but since freezing affects vitamin C content very little, frozen vegetables can give you more vitamins than supposedly fresh ones – one more argument for growing your own, or, if you cannot do that, for buying locally grown ones whenever possible. Remember, too, that incorrect cooking can severely reduce vitamin content. Our recipes ensure you get the most from all foods. On the Small Island Diet, rich in fresh food, you are unlikely to suffer any deficiencies, though in late winter and early spring you should take the usual care to eat vitamin-rich food. A deep-freeze makes such foods more readily available, but we don't have one. We bottle fruit and tomatoes, and our winter root vegetables we store naturally in cool dark places. Our beans we simply dry.

Right through winter, until we pick our first spring

salads, we still enjoy delicious daily salads which ensure our vitamin C level. Each day we ring the changes. Straight from the garden we shred cabbage and brussels sprouts, and grate swede, parsnip and celeriac; from our cool, dark store we grate carrots and beetroot. For variety we add sliced, raw leek, chopped parsley or grated horseradish – again from the garden – together with sliced raw onion and dried herbs, and of course we vary the dressings too. We also sprout wheat, mustard and cress. Sprouted beans as well are another rich source of vitamin C. There's no need to go short.

Uncooked foods are invariably richer in vitamin C than cooked ones, but we do get appreciable amounts as well from cooked greens and root vegetables, and from freshly picked leeks. It may seem strange, but if you cook vegetables the way we recommend in the recipe section, you can actually derive *more* vitamin C than eating them raw. This is because you can comfortably eat about three times more cooked cabbage, carrot, beetroot or whatever than you would want to eat raw. Since sensible cooking need only cost you about a fifth of the vitamin C content, your cooked meal should provide you with a good deal more than twice as much of the vitamin. Now, this is not to say, 'Don't eat raw vegetables', but just a reminder not to belittle properly cooked ones. Potatoes too are a good source of vitamin C, but as with all other sources, the vitamin content depreciates with storage.

Vitamin D is an essential nutrient for maintaining the level of calcium and phosphorus in the blood. It is found only in fish and animal products, including milk and butter, and so it presents no problem to us, as it could to a vegan who eats none of these. Any deficiency is more likely to occur in winter, because humans also derive the vitamin from sunlight, understandably scarce at that time.

If you take these simple precautions there should be no need to buy expensive citruses and other imported fruit and vegetables for your daily vitamin C, or for any other reason, winter or summer. In this country nowadays we can grow such a variety – including many which once only grew in warmer climates.

Eating Lower on the Food Chain

Only plant life can thrive solely on solutions of the naturally occuring mineral salts found in the soil and ocean beds. All other life – from mankind to bacteria – feeds on other living things. Some creatures, such as cows and caterpillars eat only plant life; others, such as lions and lizards, eat other creatures which themselves have grown up eating pretty well only plant life. Others prefer a diet of creatures which have eaten mostly other creatures; while still others, including mankind and pigs, generally aren't fussy – they're omnivores, eating both plant and flesh.

What emerges from all this is a chain of life in which big creatures eat smaller ones, which in turn eat plant life, which is nourished by soil or sea bed on which all life eventually depends.

Industrial man in the Rich North eats mostly at the top of this food chain. Because he does – and because of what else he does – the effects are significant, both for himself and the rest of the world.

In terms of food 'energy' he is the least efficient. At each level in the chain about ten units of food energy – fats, carbohydrates and sugar – are needed to produce one unit of food at the level above it. The energy is lost as each kind of creature grows, digests its food, keeps warm, moves around, makes love and generally goes about its business. So, the further down the chain, the more efficient is the creature. The higher up, the more its food costs: in energy, land and – in the case of mankind – money.

So much for energy: what about proteins? Here the losses and costs can escalate alarmingly. Since much land is best growing grass, and man can't eat grass, it is quite economical for him to eat, say, sheep. But once he eats animals reared substantially on food grown on land capable of growing crops he could have eaten direct, the costs soar. For example, beef cattle can eat some 20 lb of protein-rich feedstuffs to produce 1 lb of meat protein. And the performance of pigs and chickens is not so much better. This is why meat is costly. And since Britain and other industrial countries import most of their feedstuffs from the Poor South, it is one reason why people there are hungry.

Now we may not care much about world hunger, but we do – or should – care about contaminants in our diet. As we have seen, commercially grown crops are constantly sprayed and dusted with poisons in an attempt to keep ahead of pests and crop diseases. These poisons are absorbed by the crops, and also in ever increasing concentrations in the bodies of creatures at each level of the food chain. It's the same with DDT and heavy metals in fish from ocean pollution. So when man eats at the top of the food chain, he eats the most contaminated food.

It you think about it, you'll see that The Small Island Diet amounts to eating lower down the food chain. This means that it is not only cheaper – it is less contaminated with poisons and, in consequence, healthier. All the benefits of the Small Island Diet are summarized in Figure 4 (page 42).

Where to Next?

The changes we advocate are, as we have said, a starting point. Where we go from here is for each one of us to decide. More naturally reared meat and eggs not only taste better but are more enjoyable to eat because the creatures were not subjected to undue suffering. Primitive man knew that the meat from a frightened animal had inferior flavour and would not keep, and he organized his hunting methods accordingly. Our 'civilized' society acts differently, as a visit to any cattle market, or slaughter house will confirm – all the worse when the animals' journey has been long. Taste tests with vegetables have confirmed what thousands already know: that organically grown ones have more flavour. These unadulterated foods grown in healthy soil, without poisonous pesticides, weedicides and chemical fertilizers *ought* to be better for us too, and evidence now exists that they are.

In Chicago, Dr Theron Randolph, a most influential researcher on food and chemical allergies, fed people on commercially grown fruit and vegetables, and found that many of them reacted with typical allergies – not merely skin rashes and the like, but the well understood, though not commonly recognized manifestations such a depression, unexplained fatigue, headaches and temperature fluctuations. When he fed the same kinds of fruit and vegetables, grown organically without chemical contaminants, however, no reactions occurred!

It should be mentioned in passing that a proportion of people – whatever their diet – may be allergic to various foods, however grown, with or without contaminants. The principal ones which may cause reactions are processed food, sugar, instant coffee, tea, chocolate, eggs, milk and cereals. Dr Richard Mackarness recommends that anyone suspecting food allergies should have a talk with his doctor with a view to determining which food or foods are the offenders.

After reading this book you may resolve to grow more of your own unadulterated food organically in your garden, on an allotment or in someone else's unused garden; or even move to the country where you could more easily provide for more of your own needs – eggs, milk, cheese, butter, meat.

Another step to consider is bulk buying from uncontaminated sources. Once you question the point of shops selling food in dainty packages, you can think in terms of saving money at the same time as you safeguard your health. This you can do alone, or, better still, in a food co-op with friends and neighbours – a highly convivial innovation.

Having reduced their meat consumption, some people find they can get along fine without meat at all. They become vegetarians – a word which has come to include those who still eat eggs, butter and cheese, and drink milk. Some people, known as vegans, for reasons of health beliefs and conscience, decide to cut out even these items. With care over vitamins in particular, it is possible to live more healthily and enjoyably as vegetarian or vegan than the vast majority do on The Diet of Affluent Malnutrition. Many of our recipes, in fact, will suit vegetarians and vegans, with or without modification.

You might decide to reduce your tea and coffee intakes. In our recipe section you will find ideas for pleasant and harmless British-grown alternative beverages that are well worth trying. Delightful though tea and coffee are, they contain no nutrients, they are habit-forming drugs and, as with any drug, if you take them habitually or in excess, they upset the body's natural functioning. Moreover, as we have previously suggested, if you take sugar in

Figure 4 The Small Island Diet

What You Eat

MORE	LESS
	Total food intake (unless underweight)
Food grown in Britain	Imported foods (especially from countries where people are hungry)
Food grown near your home	Food grown or processed the other side of Britain
'Energy' from cereals (especially wholemeal bread), vegetables and fruit (fresh or naturally stored)	'Energy' from oil and fat (especially of animal origin) and from highly refined foods (especially sugar and white bread)
Proteins from vegetables and cereals	Proteins from meat, fish, milk, cheese and eggs
Vegetables and fruit in season when cheaper	Vegetables and fruit out of season when expensive
Natural flavours, texture and colour	Synthetic flavouring and colouring
Naturally grown food (from organic farms and from gardens and allotments where possible)	Vegetables and fruit, bred for appearance etc. rather than flavour, grown with chemicals and sprayed with poisons
	Food from factory 'farms' (especially veal, bacon, pork and non-free-range poultry and eggs)
Fresh food generally Wholefood (with roughage intact)	'Convenience' and other processed foods (especially ones containing chemical additives)
Herbs and spices	Salt
Home-grown beverages and plain water	Tea, coffee and alcohol

How You Benefit

MORE	LESS
Varied fare	Unimaginative uniformity
Pride in cooking and serving	Conditioning to advertising
Appreciation of 'feast days'	Taking treats for granted
Well-being (especially better health, slimmer appearance and clearer conscience – over world hunger and animal exploitation)	Disease (especially coronary heart disease, diabetes, cancer and tooth decay) Depression and unexplained fatigue
Money saved in household (especially by eating less, growing your own and eating more nutritious unprocessed food)	Cost (especially due to needless transportation, processing, packaging and advertising)
Money saved by nation (especially imports, N.H.S. costs, transportation, packaging and advertising)	Balance of payments problem
Certainty of future food supplies	Interrupted food supplies (especially through war, drought and famine)
FOOD GROWN FOR PEOPLE	**FOOD GROWN FOR PROFIT**

them, up goes your intake of this as well. Some people reduce their tea intake by having one cup instead of two, and cut their coffee intake by saving it for special occasions. Then you will appreciate them all the more.

The same holds good for the family joint, cream cakes, exotic fruit and vegetables and other luxuries. If you simply follow the affluent crowd and try to make every day a feast day, you heighten your expectations beyond all reasonable ability to satisfy them. On the other hand, if you save these delightful 'sins' for special occasions, such as family Sundays, birthdays and other anniversaries, Christmas or any other celebration – whether pre-arranged or spontaneous – the flavours and other pleasures are infinitely more appreciated than when you experience them all the time. And no harm done.

When we talk of restricting the regular use of imported foods – whether it is in order to enjoy special occasions all the more, or for any other reasons – it is well to bear in mind yet another benefit of a very different kind which such 'self-denial' confers. Many of the regularly eaten imported foods come from the Poor South where crops now receive an annual dosing of 800 million lb of pesticides. What is more, this figure includes deadly DDT, banned from the Rich North which now exports either the chemical or the technology in order to maintain company profits. It is not sensible to add to your daily diet such a weight of contamination to that which already exists in British food.

There are exceptions to these guidelines, however. The regular use of small amounts of imported herbs, spices, dried fruit and seeds for sprouting can make a contribution to improving palatability of simple foods which is out of proportion to their bulk and cost. A modest level of international trading in them is unlikely to harm anyone appreciably – anywhere.

You could be motivated to change the way you eat and drink because it appeals to your palate, because it can be a less expensive way, or because, as your awareness of where it comes from expands, so you seek to allay your conscience. Alternatively you might put health above all these considerations.

Finally you might be influenced to consider wider

issues and the longer term future – Britain's ability to feed herself in a progressively less supportive environment. By changing gradually to The Small Island Diet today, you will be agreeably and beneficially accustoming yourself to a way of eating which may be inevitable tomorrow. And tomorrow may come sooner than any of us expect.

3
TOWARDS A MORE SELF-SUFFICIENT BRITAIN

Britain now imports about half her food. Whether the figure is a good deal more than half, or rather less, depends on how you do the sums – or, more accurately, on how you interpret the complex figures produced by the Ministry of Agriculture, Fisheries and Food (MAFF). Our own interpretation is that Officialdom paints too rosy a picture. By the time you've taken account of the feedstuffs Britain imports and several other factors, such as re-exports of high-priced processed food, we all show up to be a good deal more dependent on the rest of the world than official figures imply – and far more than is good for us.

On one count, however, there is no ambiguity. Living on a Diet of Affluent Malnutrition, Britain imports inordinate amounts of certain foods and beverages which we could all quite happily consume less of; and we import unconscionable quantities of others which we could perfectly well grow here. Figure 5 overleaf shows what we mean. For example, in 1980 on six items alone, we got through £3,100 million – just meat, fruit, vegetables, coffee, tea and cocoa – and that impressive sum will be very much higher today.

It's not that MAFF is unaware of the danger. In its publication 'Farming and the Nation' it states that 'there is a real argument ... to maintain the security of some of our basic food supplies by increasing the proportion produced at home.' MAFF is even mindful that grain is the staple food of people in the Poor South, for it adds, '... if increased imports of grain for livestock production make it scarcer or more expensive for them, such imports should where possible be avoided.'

MAFF states the problem plainly, but characteristically fails to come out with an implemented strategy to enable British farmers willingly to work towards solving it. So change happens all too slowly.

Other people, however, have been active. Back in 1975 two authorities separately addressed themselves to the problem: Dr Kenneth Blaxter, director of Rowett Research Institute, Aberdeen; and Kenneth Mellanby, one-time head of Rothamsted Research Station. Since then a number of others have followed suit, including Professor J.C. Bowman with his team at the Centre for Agricultural Strategy, Reading; and Robert Vale, of the Open University's Technology Policy Group.

Figure 5 The Food, Feed and Drink We Import (1980)

	£ million
Meat and meat products	1226
Live animals	105
Dairy products and eggs	500
Fish and fish products	349
Cereals and cereal products	604
Fruit and vegetables	1240
Sugar and sugar products	403
Coffee, tea and cocoa	677
Miscellaneous	750
Animal feedstuffs	249
Total food and feed	6103

Small Island Farming

Naturally enough, anyone working independently on the problem of enabling Britain to become more self-sufficient in food will come up with his own ideas. Nevertheless, if you examine the various proposals, you discover that they have plenty in common. Some are pretty radical, others more conservative. As authors we take the view that, while Government should lead, change will only be effective when the time is ripe and the people recognize the need for change. Anything else, unless dictatorially imposed, is simply swimming against the tide – and you know where that gets you. Change, therefore, should be no faster than enlightened people are willing to accept, no more drastic than the situation demands. We have already portrayed a vision of the future: the speed and extent of change in Britain should be determined by the anticipated rate and degree of change beyond her shores. This book aims to enlighten – the first step.

Figure 6   How Self-Sufficient Are We?

Percentage of average annual consumption represented by home production (1979):

Crops:
Wheat	75
Barley	106
Oats	90
Oilseed rape	55
Sugar	47
Potatoes	92
Apples	49
Pears	58
Tomatoes	40

Livestock products:
Beef and veal	86
Mutton and lamb	60
Pork	98
Bacon and ham	41
Poultry meat	99
Eggs	102
Liquid milk	100
Cream	97
Butter	47
Cheese	65

Note: above livestock product percentages do not take into account feedstuffs imported to produce the food and drink; more than 100% indicates that we export.

Central to Small Island Farming is a different view about the kind of cattle we shall keep and the way to feed them. You may see more dairy cattle on the landscape –

Jerseys or maybe the ousted Dairy Shorthorn – and they will have to thrive much as they used to do: chiefly on pasture and fodder crops – such as roots and kale – but supplemented with home-grown feedstuffs, notably bulky by-products we ourselves can't eat – from sugar beet and edible oil extraction, from breweries and other activities. No more will they get imported fishmeal and soya bean meal. There are two chief reasons why we may need extra dairy cattle. On bulkier, more natural – and healthier – feed, without force-feeding with excessive concentrates, each animal will produce less; and we shall need extra milk to make the butter and cheese which we shall no longer be importing.

We shall wind down our pure beef herds so that they produce just enough bulls to inseminate a proportion of our dairy cows to produce dairy-beef cross calves. In effect, beef farming will be predominantly a by-product of dairy farming as it used to be and the calves will be fattened on pretty much the same diet as their mums. In fact, something like this is already happening, but the trend will be intensified.

We may run rather more sheep than now, and they will get much the same treatment. You'll be seeing most of them grazing the rougher and upland pastures on which they thrive, and in order to release the better pasture for cattle which are more choosy.

Pig numbers too may decline and they will get none of their feed as imported feedstuffs, rather less of it as home-grown barley meal, and much more as those by-products which people are less able or willing to eat, as well as small potatoes, whey and the millions of tons of swill from cities currently wasted, though safe to feed if sterilized.

If we are going to feed our livestock from our own farms, rather than farms abroad, and if we plan to stop importing shiploads of North American wheat for our bread, we shall need plenty of arable land on which to grow cereals, potatoes and other crops. We may also have to find more arable land to grow more sugar beet, for although the Small Island Diet means eating less sugar, what we do eat must likewise come from our own farms. One important crop which needs no extra land is honey, which can healthfully replace a useful amount of sugar. There is scope to increase British honey production many times over. There is another important crop we have to find room for, one which farmers have been growing more readily of late, and now assumes supreme importance if we are to realise our aims. The crop is oilseed rape, one of the few plants to grow in temperate climates and yield worthwhile amounts of edible oil. This crop we shall need in abundance to help replace imported oil extracted from peanuts, soya beans, and so on.

Figure 7 Oilseed Rape

With our sheep moved chiefly to steeper, rougher land and with fewer cattle overall, much of our flatter, more fertile land will be released for cropping – not relentlessly year after year, but as part of a fertility-restoring rotation, which includes a spell as pasture after a succession of years growing varied crops – as in the best farming tradition.

We shall need more land too for extra vegetables and fruit, but much of this can come from the 292,000 acres, mostly on the fringes of cities and towns, currently under-used, or unused, which will be made available for smallholders and market gardeners – applicants are already queuing for such land. Allotments and gardens will also play their part, though the main responsibility of increasing food production will be squarely on the shoulders of the experienced farmer and market gardener.

As in all walks of life, some farmers are better than others; in consequence some land grows more food than other land – even though it is no more fertile. The less productive farmers will be helped to match the performance of their more accomplished neighbours. A judicious blend of incentives and penalties worked effectively during the critical years of the Second World War, and no doubt would work again. There is no lack of evidence that farmers with small farms achieve higher yields on each acre than those with larger farms. This evidence cannot be disregarded, for land is scarce and able-bodied people are not. The trend to ever-larger farms, as neighbour swallows neighbour, will have to be reversed.

Neither can we ignore the threat to the quality of food and the land's future fertility by persistent overdosing with pesticides and chemical fertilizers. After all, we are part of nature, not separate. The land is our best friend. Would you poison your best friend? Given the will to do so, there is no reason at all why the dangerous trend to increasing dependence on chemical, often poisonous, pesticides and fertilizers should not be halted and reversed. Farmers and gardeners could use far more organic fertilizers than they do now. Farm slurry, which is now regarded as a nuisance and pollutant, could be returned to the land. Moreover, just as city food waste could become feedstuffs, city garbage and sewage – a similar embarrassment – could be returned to the land as high grade manure. If the Chinese can do it, so can we!

Once the morality of growing food for people rather than for profit is understood, so the concept of *stewardship* rather than ownership of land should follow naturally. What counts is the *relationship* between people and the land they work. The accountant-farmer, who becomes increasingly dependent on banks and petrochemical companies, who equips his employees with massive tractors in which they work in unrelieved monotony, high above the ground in cabs equipped with stereo radios, feels differently about land and livestock compared with the family farmer and his few acres. Agribusiness exploits the land; the true farmer nurtures it. The two do not live in the same world.

The Countryside Revived

Robert Vale envisages three types of farming: the first will be fairly large scale arable farming to grow our wheat, oats, barley, hops, sugar beet and oilseed rape; the second will be intensive vegetable growing – the market gardeners and the important 'allotment sector'; while the third will be livestock farming, 'akin to the kind of smallholding practised by peasant farmers in many parts of the world,' as he puts it. These farmers will also manage orchards and grow fodder crops, though not grain. In all three types of farming, animal manure and other organic wastes from town and country will be returned to enrich the land, rather than contribute to pollution problems – as happens now.

Whatever the farming systems used, a more self-sufficient Britain will need more families living on the land – a development capable of solving more problems than it might create. In Britain now, a mere 2.7 per cent of the workforce is in agriculture – the lowest in the EEC, where the average is 9.7 per cent, where Eire has 24.3 per cent on the land and Germany 7.3 per cent. So even if we substantially increased our agricultural workforce we wouldn't exactly be returning to a pre-industrial way of life! On the contrary, any increase would provide work which city-based industry is patently failing to offer. Decentralization would be stimulated as industry tended to follow the new farm families, in order to provide for local needs. We would witness a dying countryside revived.

Now some people will doubtless view any such changes with dismay, envisaging a countryside spattered with red brick bungalows and small industries. Others however will bear in mind that much of the countryside will be unaffected, and where it is changed, they will picture houses built in local styles with local materials, set among trees and gardens. They may even prefer a countryside dominated by working farm families to one where retired couples, commuters and holiday homes predominate.

Some will wring their hands at the costs involved. Food will cost more, they'll point out. The capital costs of improving farms, creating new ones, relocating families and re-siting industries will cripple the nation. And it all smacks of dictatorship! There is another side, however. Some of the higher food costs would be offset: less produce would be wastefully hauled to central markets and then sent back to where it came from; and, with locally grown food meeting local demands, food processing costs would be cut. The extra employment created would mean savings in unemployment benefits. But most significant of all would be the savings achieved by cutting food imports – over £3,000 million each year on 'temperate climate foods' – those we could grow here but don't; together with several more hundred millions on imported livestock feed, even more on tropical 'luxuries'; and a useful saving in imported fertilizers.

As for the 'dictatorship' charge, we have already made our views clear on the speed and extent of change: when it is needed, enlightened people will seek it – even if it involves land reform; even if it means stopping the current loss of over 120,000 acres of our best farmland every year to housing and industry; even if it requires a National Food Policy to relate food production to what people need, rather than to what they are persuaded to want ... and so on.

Edmund Burke once said: 'For the triumph of evil it is only necessary that good men do nothing'. So we can't expect land reform, a halt to land losses through development, *caring* systems of animal and crop husbandry and a food policy which puts people before profit to emerge unless enlightened people make appropriate noises. Ideas for becoming involved in activities to promote desirable change will be found in our Ideas for Action.

Britain has the land – the best in the world. We have let it dwindle to about half an acre for each person – half what it was ninety years ago – but if we farm it well and lovingly it will feed us – provided that we hang on to what's left. Britain has the farmers. Many of those displaced would return from the cities given the incentives. Countless thousands of young people – able-bodied, eager to learn

Figure 8 How Britain is Farmed

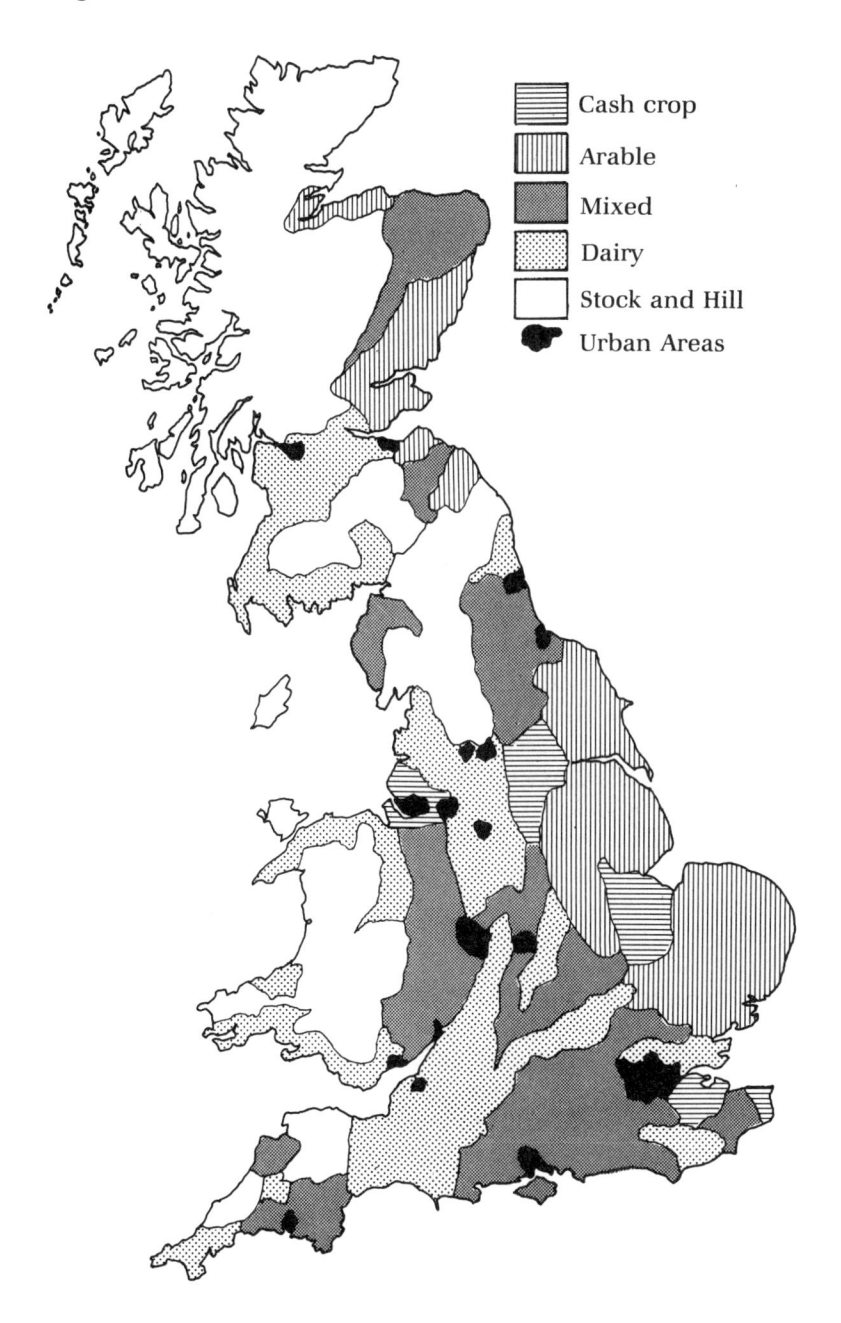

and appalled by the prospect of factory and office life – would join them given the chance. Britain has the wealth. In comparison with our 3,200 million Poor South neighbours – each with an income roughly equal to the cost of a new set of tyres for the family car – we rate as oil sheiks. We have a choice: to squander our oil-based wealth; or to direct resources to where they will ensure the most precious and basic of all our needs: nutritious, unadulterated, uncontaminated food, grown without depriving others.

Won't the Poor Get Poorer?
If Britain gradually reduced her imports of food from Poor South countries where people are hungry, the answer to this vital question would be 'no'. Indeed, in time they could well be better off.

Now as authors we appreciate that not everyone is deeply concerned with the subject of world poverty and hunger; we can also understand that many readers would feel uncomfortable to be confronted by truths which seem to implicate them as condoning, or even aggravating, other people's plight – however unwittingly. To them we offer reassurance that The Small Island Diet has no 'harmful side-effects', and we suggest they skip the rest of this chapter.

To others, whose equally understandable reaction is to doubt us, or who do feel deep concern, or who welcome a debate with a touch of *planetary* – as opposed to *partisan* – politics anyway, we extend a welcome to stay with us for the next few pages. Causes and cures of world poverty and hunger are clearly an immensely complex subject, so we must ask forgiveness if lack of space means over-simplifying. Nevertheless, we feel bound to offer some explanation of the probable consequences if Britain became more nearly self-sufficient in food. It would, after all, be grossly improper to propose a policy which stood to benefit Britain, and then for us to leave an impression that we had done so, aware that it would be at the expense of others; or that we had not taken the trouble to find out what might happen. We should also add that what follows is based, neither on hunch, nor blind optimism, but on the findings of considerable research.

TOWARDS A MORE SELF-SUFFICIENT BRITAIN   57

Figure 9   Rich North and Poor South

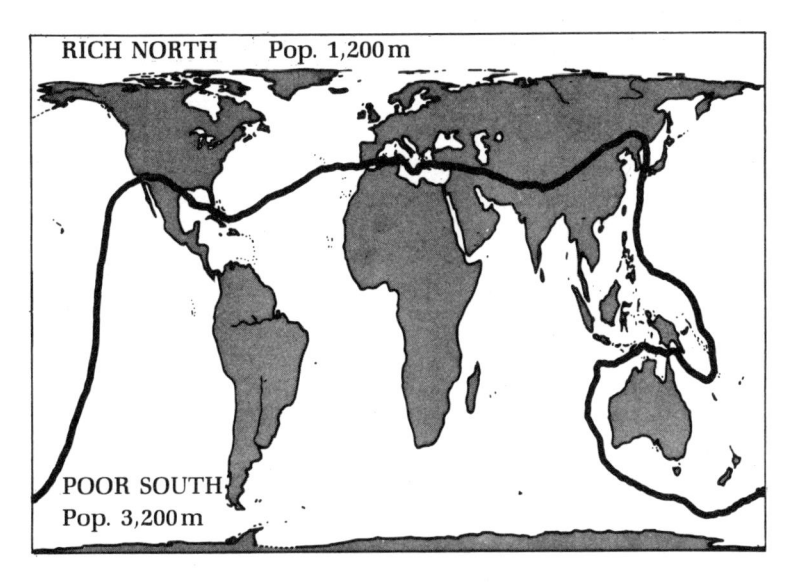

[Map: RICH NORTH Pop. 1,200m / POOR SOUTH Pop. 3,200m]

Map by courtesy of Dr Arno Peters of the University of Bremen.

The world's people can be roughly divided into 'developed' and 'developing nations'. The latter have come to be known collectively as The Third World – the first and second being capitalist and communist, while the third represents the non-aligned nations. In distinguishing between rich and poor, however, political differences have now become less relevant than, for example, income per head of population. Even this measure becomes a crude generalisation however when, as in South America, it may conceal a misleading concentration of wealth among a few and extreme poverty for many. No arbitrary measure of universal human well-being therefore will ever be perfect, but the terms 'Rich North and 'Poor South' have gained increasing acceptance, despite the obvious anomalies of Southern Africa and the Antipodes. We have used them throughout this book as the most appropriate in discussing trans-world movements of food. (This map is based on a projection of Arno Peters to convey a better indication of relative land areas – especially those of the Poor South – than the customary Mercator's projection.)

The Myth of Food Shortage

At present the world is neither short of food, nor land on which to grow it. Poverty is the cause of hunger. Food 'flows' not to where there is most need, but to where there is most money. In consequence, while many eat too much, even more eat too little. If food were more equably distributed, and waste reduced, there would be more than enough for everyone, even for many years to come.

In very many Southern countries where hunger is widespread the most fertile land is farmed, not by small farmers, but by wealthy landowners and multi-national corporations. This land grows little, if any, food for local consumption. Instead, most of its produce is exported to Britain and other countries in the Rich North; a high proportion as food for farm livestock, rather than for Northern people to eat directly. The same land also grows non-food export crops, such as cotton, rubber, jute, coffee, tea and tobacco.

Countries in the Poor South retain only a small share of the profits made by multinational companies from all these exports. Most of this is used to benefit the countries' small ruling elite and middle-class, and to build and try to maintain modern cities and industrial projects, inappropriately modelled on the Rich North.

For these and other reasons, the rest of the people remain poor. Unemployment commonly runs at 30 per cent or more and under-nutrition predominates. Large numbers of people migrate constantly from the country to the cities' outskirts where they live in shacks made from scrap, without electricity, water or sewerage. They leave the countryside in search of food and work. Of those who remain in the countryside, some find jobs at very low wages on the big farm estates, though each year jobs are harder to find as machinery replaces people. Some find seasonal migratory work of a kind which machines are not yet able to do.

The small farmers who still cling to their land live precariously. They cannot compete with the big farmers, because although they have no lack of knowledge, skills and incentive, they lack capital, basic implements and roads to markets. By the time they have paid their taxes, rent and debt interest *in kind*, they often have no food for their families, let alone a surplus to sell. Sometimes they sell out to rich neighbours; sometimes they are driven off at gunpoint; sometimes they just walk away. Whatever happens only three courses remain open to them: to move and become subsistence farmers on poorer land, too steep, eroding or inaccessible to interest the wealthy; to seek work in the country or – more often – in the cities, and so swell the queues for work and food. Whatever happens, the food which they might have grown for the hungry, is not grown. They become *liabilities* instead of assets.

The Good Earth grows enough food as *grain alone* to feed everyone on it 2 lb a head each day, which, though monotonous, is a diet as nourishing as that of any well-fed Northerner – and far better balanced. In practice, much of that grain is wasted. Over one third of it is fed to livestock for meat destined for Northern tables. Why wasted? Because livestock 'shrink' 1,800 lb of grain to produce 250 lb of meat. More sensibly, the hungry eat grain as it is!

As we can see, then, there is no shortage of food. The poor simply cannot afford the prices which British farmers can afford to pay. In monetary terms it is more attractive to feed farm livestock than people; more attractive to grow luxury tropical crops for export than staple food crops for indigenous people; more attractive to grow – *non-food* crops, even though the land could grow food equally well. In consequence the governments of many Southern countries, are forced to import food! The Poor South today is a *net importer* of food from the Rich North.

How It Came About
To understand how this has come about we have to look at the past. The centuries have witnessed a steady and growing transfer of wealth from South to North. The belief has grown that the God-given role of the hot countries is to be providers of food and other crops to the industrial countries of the temperate zones. The early colonists, set in motion the transfer chiefly by acquiring land previously farmed by villagers. They were not all ogres however: mostly they acted – as we all do – from self-interest, but much of the time they genuinely believed they were acting in the best interests of the people whose cultures they were destroying. Not that these cultures were perfect, but

they had spawned no vast cities, and in the smaller, face-to-face communities, relying on long-established farming practices, the poor were always fed.

Colonialism was succeeded by economic invasion from the North, stimulated by the need for new export markets, but latterly even more strongly by the international scramble for the resources on which affluent industrial economies have come to depend – oil, essential metals and food. In this trend, the most significant development has been the growth of multinational companies, many of whose Annual Turnovers exceed the Gross National Products of Poor South countries where they operate.

The disappearance of colonialism has witnessed a decline rather than improvement in living standards in the Poor South, a decline for which population explosion has commonly been blamed; but since there is no food shortage, and the South is still the repository for most of the world's remaining important natural resources, one must seek other reasons for the decline. There are many, of course, but two predominate. Firstly, the governments of countries in the South tend not to identify closely with the majority of their own people. They have closer links with wealthy local landowners, with their country's small middle-class, and with their peers in the North – including multinational executives. Secondly, the international monetary system favours those Northern countries which hold the most wealth and power, for predictably it is they who make the rules.

Can It Be Changed?

Putting the world to rights lies outside the scope of this book, no matter how concerned its authors and readers may be about the world's ills. Nevertheless we can take a look at the practice of international trading in staple foods which does fall within its scope.

Consider for a moment conditions in some countries from where Britain imports staple foods. We buy over 80 per cent of our corned beef from South America where half the children under the age of six live in critical poverty and under-nutrition. In the Caribbean, from where we import much of our sugar and bananas, half the farmland is planted to cash crops, yet seven in every ten children are under-nourished, and two thirds of the region's food has to be imported. From the Sahel, in North Africa, we import peanuts for cattle feed, yet in the mid-seventies drought, exports of this food crop actually rose, while its people starved to death in thousands.

It is an uncomfortable truth that so long as we in Britain continue eating food from countries where hunger is widespread, or eat meat fattened on feedstuffs they have grown, we are doing nothing to help the hungry.

It is an equally uncomfortable dilemma that if Britain alone stopped, other countries would take up the slack. Prices paid for Southern food might fall marginally overall, and some crops in some countries would be affected more than others, but unilateral action by us would neither make the general situation significantly better or worse. Things won't improve however by doing nothing. On their own, unaided, people in Poor South countries are virtually powerless, for they lack such resources as literacy, knowledge of their legal rights, money and *energy* – prolonged hunger is debilitating.

So what can the Rich North do?

To the best of their ability, Oxfam, War on Want and other voluntary agencies are already providing these desperately needed resources – as field workers, literature, legal aid, appropriate technology and hope. It is a mere trickle, but more effective than any flood of inappropriate official aid, conventionally tied to trade and maintaining the *status quo*. There is a need for concerned people to support such work and to open national debates, especially in the media, so that people may know of the nature of continuing hunger, and their own connection with it. It would then be possible to identify where Northern policies, governmental and commercial, are hindering reforms so that corrective action might follow.

National debates would need to be followed by international debates: *Collective* action to work towards national self-sufficiency in food would be more effective than unilateral action. Such action could represent a turning point, for history provides a precedent. In the slump of the thirties, when world food prices fell, countless foreign landowners in the Poor South sold out once the profit vanished. This enabled small farmers to move in and grow food for themselves and their compatriots.

So much for any rudimentary stimulus from the North. What could be achieved in the South?

Land redistribution is the key. However, essential land tenure reform will not come about while governments there depend on support of landowners, local and foreign. Nevertheless, nothing is immutable: if attempts at reform in the South can be thwarted by action from the North – Chile is the prime example – with more enlightened Northern motives, they can instead be *encouraged.* A literate populace motivated by the restoration of its rights is any emerging democracy's strongest ally.

If help from the North were to facilitate a transfer of decision-making to the people, certainly it would have to be accompanied by a measure of decentralization. This is important, for when people work for themselves, for family and community, they produce far more than when working for remote employers. Thus, small farms invariably produce more than large ones, for what counts most is *the relationship between people and land.* In other words, putting food for people before food for profit. If decisions were made according to this principle, food would be exported *only* after the needs of the people had been met.

In such a changed political and economic climate, the Poor South's present frenetic hunt for foreign exchange would lose its impetus. A country would rely more upon the capital inherent in the energies of a hitherto unemployed workforce – well-fed and hopeful for the first time in years. Some funds might conceivably flow in from a reformed international monetary system, spurred to transfer wealth back to the South from where it was taken. If so, any such aid, free from ties, would be channelled – not so much to cities' centres as in the past – but to rural areas to grow more food than before, on small farms with indigenous, labour-intensive practices, and so reverse the migration to the cities.

It was a remarkably similar model which China adopted after the sudden withdrawal of Soviet technological aid – a model which put an end to recurrent famines and degrading poverty in that unique country of the Poor South where a quarter of the world's population lives.

The scenario outlined is of course hedged with 'ifs and buts'. Profound changes in the Poor South are already under way, but the *status quo* is stubbornly resilient. Whatever the outcome of the struggle however, the prospects for Britain's food will still depend on the *total* environment. And as we saw at the beginning, that is dominated by the amount of farmland for each person in the world, the number of people it has to feed, and Britain's ability to buy any surplus food from beyond her shores. Taking all these into account, it would appear sensible for Britain to practise what we have preached for *all* countries: to avoid dependence on others by growing as much of her own food as she reasonably can.

PART TWO

4
STEPS TO CREATIVITY

You can begin to follow The Small Island Diet whether you live in the city or the country. Although your own garden or allotment makes it easier, neither is essential. In fact we evolved and practised The Diet without any difficulty over a period of two years while we lived in a London basement flat with neither. Let's make one thing absolutely clear: you don't have to live in the country, so The Diet isn't just for people there who have enough land to aim for self-sufficiency. For much of our lives we had been farmers, and after our two years evolving The Small Island Diet we returned to the country. We now grow as much of our own food as makes sense, but our vegetable patch isn't much larger than most city allotments.

We grow our vegetables in the middle of an eight-acre smallholding with the kind of terrain which even a family farmer would think twice about, and agribusiness would promptly write off – which is why it was derelict and the house virtually a ruin when we came to it some six years ago. Most of the land around the 'allotment' is too steep, stony or shady to grow crops, so we have planted some of it to orchard, some to trees and sown the rest to pasture, except for an acre left as wilderness. We keep a few hens for eggs, a couple of goats for milk and cheese, and a small flock of sheep for meat and wool. Most of this produce is a surplus for sale or barter to provide us with food we cannot really grow – such as cereals because the climate is too damp. What food we do buy usually comes in bulk: we buy sacks of wheat from a nearby farm, which we grind to make wholemeal flour for our own bread.

Since we grow most of our own fuel too and live

frugally, we do not need to earn so much money as do most people. Enough for our needs and wants comes from writing, public speaking and broadcasting. This way of life is neither secure nor easy, but it seems to us a less exploitative one, with rewards which have little to do with money. Because it is an unusual way to live, many people, who live similarly or would like to, have come to see it these past six years, and their reactions to our beliefs, and to the hundreds of meals we have provided, have prompted us to write this book.

Growing Your Own

There is so much to be said for growing your own vegetables – and fruit too if you have room – that if you have no garden of your own we do urge you to strive for an allotment. Local councils have a legal obligation to provide them for all applicants and it is necessary to lobby them constantly. Meanwhile you may be able to grow food in someone's unused garden, sharing with the owner some of your harvest. If this fails, all is not lost, for you can usually grow some fresh food on window sills, on the roof or a patio, and even indoors, not only where there is light, but in the darkness of cupboards or a cellar where a few crops thrive.

There are at least nine good reasons for growing your own.

• Economy: you can expect a return of 1,000 per cent on your investment in seeds. But this isn't all: you may not have worked out that every £100 of produce you grow is really worth about £150 if you take into account the income tax you probably have to pay before you can take home the £100 you would otherwise have to spend at the greengrocer or supermarket.

• Convenience: less shopping and queueing: easy to cater for unexpected guests.

• Freshness: hence more enjoyable and better for you, especially in vitamins.

• Flavour: your fruit and vegetables will also taste better because you can grow varieties bred for flavour. Commercial growers have been forced to concentrate on ones bred to resist diseases; for uniform ripening to suit harvesting machines; for thick skins to travel long distances; for colours with 'eye-appeal'; for heavy yields to boost profits ... just about everything except flavour! Moreover, because they overdose crops with chemical fertilizers to force even higher yields, the quickly grown, sappy produce often lacks both flavour and texture.

• Safer: no poisonous sprays.

• Variety: shops cater for majority tastes, but you can be adventurous. Plant breeders may have sinned, but they have atoned by developing varieties of 'hot country' fruit and vegetables which were once impossible or chancy, but now grow well in Britain, some of them even outdoors without glass. Sweet corn, peppers, melons, aubergines, oranges and lemons, peaches, nectarines, apricots and almonds ... the list is growing, and as it does, so the excuse to import diminishes.

• Enjoyable: a fascinating hobby, easy, with few ties.

• Exercise: the fresh air and exertion will do you a power of good.

• Aesthetics: a house surrounded with – and even filled with – growing plants reminds us of our links with nature, and looks beautiful.

In a host of ways, then, it pays to grow your own. The question is 'what?' Aim to grow vegetables that yield the most for every square foot of land they occupy, and avoid those which are tricky to grow. High yielders include beans (broad, dwarf and runner), beetroot, carrots, lettuce, marrows, onions, spinach, swiss chard and tomatoes. None of these is difficult, except perhaps tomatoes in some years. Also easy to grow are kale, leeks, parsnips, swedes, turnips and radishes. Unless you have plenty of land, forget maincrop potatoes and only grow earlies. Food normally grown out of doors may also grow indoors, such as courgettes, cucumbers, various herbs, lettuce, chicory, mushrooms, salsify, radishes, strawberries and tomatoes. You can also grow indoors sprouted wheat, alfalfa, mung beans, and mustard and cress.

We have already touched on the question of storing

vegetables, so, at the time you sow, think ahead to harvesting and afterwards. Remember that you can store carrots and beetroot in boxes of peat or sand, apples in trays, onions strung up or hung up in old tights – all where it's cool and dry. We'll deal with freezing presently.

Figure 10 lists most vegetables you can grow out of doors in a fair-sized plot. It shows when you can expect to eat them fresh, and when you can eat them from natural storage – that is neither bottled, heat-dried nor frozen.

Figure 10 How to Eat Delicious Vegetables and Fruit All-Year-Round (Outdoor-Grown and Stored Naturally)

Notes: All dates are for southern latitudes; subtract as you go north. By 'natural storage' we mean neither heated (ie bottled or oven-dried) nor frozen.

Storage Key:

C means clamp or box   G means leave in ground
D means dry   S means store in cool, dry room

Crop	Fresh	Stored naturally
VEGETABLES		
Artichoke, globe	June-Aug	
Artichoke, jerusalem	Nov-Jan	(G)
Asparagus	Apr-June	
Beans		
Broad	June-July	All year (D)
Daffa (tic)	Aug-Oct	All year (D)
French	July-Oct	
Haricot	Aug-Sept	All year (D)
Runner	July-Oct	All year (D) (bean only)
Beetroot	July-Oct	Nov-May (C)
Beet Spinach	Sept-Dec	
Broccoli, Heading	Oct-May	
Broccoli, Sprouting	Dec-May	
Brussels sprouts	Oct-March	
Brussels sprouts (tops)	March-Apr	
Cabbage	All year	
Cauliflower	Apr-Nov	
Celeriac	Oct-March	(G)
Celery	Sept-Nov	

Crop	Fresh	Stored naturally
VEGETABLES (contd)		
Chicory	Nov-May	
Corn, Sweet	Aug-Sept	
Cucumber (burpless)	July-Oct	
Kale (curly)	Nov-Apr	
Khol-rabi	July-Nov	
Leek	Oct-Apr	(G)
Lettuce	Apr-Nov	
Marrows	July-Oct	Oct-Jan (S)
Onions	July-Sept	Oct-Apr (S)
Onions, (Spring)	Feb-Sept	
Parsley	All year	(D)
Parsnip	Nov-March	(G) or (C) later
Peppers	Aug-Sept	
Peas	June-Sept	(D)
Peas, Sugar or Mange Tout	June-Sept	
Potatoes, Early	June-Oct	
Potatoes, Maincrop	Sept-Oct	(C)
Pumpkin	Aug-Sept	Oct-March (S)
Radishes	May-Oct	
Salsify	Nov-Apr	(G)
Shallots	June-July	(Aug-Apr) (S)
Spinach	All year	
Swiss Chard	All year	
Swedes	July-Feb	(C) (G)
Tomatoes	Aug-Oct	
Turnips	June-March	(C)
SOFT FRUITS		
Blackberries	July-Sept	
Blackcurrants	June-Aug	
Gooseberries	June and Aug	
Loganberries	July-Aug	
Raspberries	June-Nov	
Redcurrants (and white currants)	July	
Strawberries	June-Nov	
TOP FRUITS		
Apples	Aug-Nov	Nov-March (S)
Cherries	June-July	
Figs	Aug-Sept	
Peaches (and nectarines)	July-Sept	
Pears	Aug-Nov	Nov-Jan (S)
Plums (and damsons, gages)	July-Oct	

Equipping Your Kitchen

To follow the Small Island Diet does not demand a high technology kitchen. Unless you're blessed with an old-fashioned cool pantry, a refrigerator today seems to have become obligatory, but we contend that a deep-freeze must remain an optional extra. As we have said, we do not have one, chiefly because between us we eat so little meat, but also because, with a Rayburn cooker, which burns mostly wood, bottling fruit is inexpensive for us. Besides the purchase cost of a freezer you must consider the running cost, which is much higher than that of a refrigerator. There are benefits of course, especially during times of glut in the fruit and vegetable garden, and you can be more care-free about vitamin intake in winter.

We teeter on the edge of buying one, but what usually decides us against – apart from the cost and an overall aversion to excess technology in the kitchen and beyond – is the prospect of losing the joy of tasting fruit and vegetables when they come in season. Something to do with the 'celebration factor' we mentioned earlier – the looking forward and then the delightful shock to taste buds not cloyed by habit. Before we consider buying we shall probably try sharing with a neighbour – an idea which abounds with even wider possibilities.

We have a largish 'Atlas' flour grinder, because we prefer bread baked from freshly ground flour. With our steady stream of visitors, we appreciate its size, eminently suitable for a large family, though smaller models by other makers are available. Although we consider most kitchen electrical gadgets unnecessary, our well-made blender proves invaluable for quick soups made from left-overs and for sauces. It has a small grinder attachment, also useful. As for massive mixers, we say 'no thanks'. A pressure cooker can save time and fuel – plenty of makes to choose from, but aim for a large one, for what holds a lot holds a little.

What else might you find useful for the sort of preparation and cooking that fresh food demands but processed food does not? Heavy fry pans and heavy based enamel or cast iron pans – or if you can afford them, stainless steel pans; oven-to-table ware. Many doctors and dieticians suggest not using aluminium for cooking, out of concern about aluminium poisoning; a Chinese cooking pan – the 'work'; plenty of different sized mixing bowls with lids, so that you can use them for storage in fridge or pantry; extra-large bowls for mixing salads; a pestle and mortar, some sieves, a ladle with holes or a slotted spoon; a garlic crusher, a pepper mill; a really good stainless steel, square grater – expensive but it will not discolour your fruit and vegetables, and will last a lifetime; for a large family we recommend a French Mouli grater; a Chinese or Japanese vegetable scrubbing brush, or failing that, an old-fashioned nailbrush; lots of wooden forks and spoons, including wide, flat ones, and spatulas too – bamboo if possible; and plenty of sharp, stainless steel knives.

Attitudes
The Small Island Diet is not just a matter of eating more of this and less of that. It implies that we all change our *attitudes* to food; looking upon it as more than fuel and indulgence, sparing a few moments before preparing and cooking food, and again before eating, to reflect on the astonishing fertility and growth which makes it possible. Food – which we too often take for granted – is the work of many hands and many miracles for which we both give thanks.

To feel relaxed while eating helps digestion; this is well known to doctors, as too is the value of chewing as opposed to 'bolting' food. Since so much effort and care went into the food to grow it, transport, prepare and cook it, we believe that it deserves some attention while it is eaten, certainly not in silence, yet – for our digestion's sake – not in discordant argument either.

We believe that good food can only be prepared when the person cooking is in a good frame of mind, neither impatient nor resentful, nor in any way uncaring. The Small Island Diet will demand of the cook, more time spent in the kitchen than has become customary. We hope that if this time passes in an agreeable frame of mind, it is time well spent, and rewarded by the well-being and appreciation of those who enjoy the meal. There is, after all, justified pride in satisfying one's skill as a cook to serve really good, pure food, especially if at least some of it is home-grown. It is a totally different experience from simply following the instructions on the side of a packet, and so becoming a mere appendage to the food industry, 'programmed' to eat what the TV commercials proclaim.

It is difficult not to become 'programmed'. Everything sounds so easy; 'just add water, pop under the microwave (or whatever) and serve in a few minutes'. Yet there is one important thing the persuaders in the food industry omit to mention: the *hidden* price. This is the risk to health from food contaminants in the form of residual, toxic pesticides and herbicides regularly used in growing the cereals and vegetables used by the food industry; as well as the subsequent inadequately tested chemical additives which make their time-saving foods possible. *The Lancet* expressed appropriate concern in an editorial in 1979 which said, 'The question of the ultimate effect of food additives on man is still unanswered.'

Most people have adapted to the natural changes in mankind's diet over millenia. Minor quantities of poisons are present in many natural foods and all but a minority of us have adapted to cope with them. However, the sudden introduction of chemicals which do not occur naturally in food poses a different problem. In all probability a high proportion of us just aren't capable of adapting to them.

The problem takes two forms: present and future. Even today the cause of disease still baffles doctors, for it is clearly not germs and bacteria alone. There are clues, however, and one clue concerns these food contaminants, for it is known that they produce allergic reactions. Any body tissues so affected are ideal seedbeds for germs and bacteria: to quote just one example, a mild asthma can lead to chronic bronchitis, which can kill – and does. If the skin and lungs can be affected, there is no reason why, in some people the brain should not also be affected, with consequent mental disturbances and diseases. These are aspects of a present problem which receive less attention than straightforward poisoning.

The future problem, as we have pointed out, is more insidious; it is the risk to health from slowly but steadily accumulating toxins and carcinogens in the body, the effects of which only time will reveal. Children will be the most likely victims.

About the Recipes

Ours is not a book to teach cookery. We know that most of our readers will be capable cooks. We aim to restore to them the right to creativity in their kitchens – an authority eroded by the printed packet. We hope to show that with natural, and predominantly British-grown ingredients – and imaginations stimulated by challenge – meals can become *safe* again at the same time as they regain their flavour and variety.

Over the years we have both become wary of 'philosophies' which sound or read convincing when propounded, but leave us in mid-air when the time comes to put them into practice. When we planned this book we were determined that this would not happen. We have already indicated ways in which any interested reader may become involved with making Britain more self-supporting in food – from 'growing his own' to pressure group activity. Similarly we have outlined broadly how any person concerned with the problem of world hunger may become an activist – to change from being part of the problem to becoming part of the solution! The 'Ideas for Action' section at the end of the book lists names and addresses to contact.

We now approach the part of the book where you can take practical steps yourself to begin following The Small Island Diet. All the recipes which follow are ones we use regularly. Each has to satisfy at least one of fourteen stringent criteria to deserve inclusion.

The criteria are:

- No commercially processed ingredients
- Minimum of imported essential staple foods
- Cooking well the foods commonly spoiled
- Use of unfamiliar ingredients
- Use of surpluses during gluts
- Ways of eating well during seasonal shortages
- Use of products from a small farm
- Meatless dishes
- Meat and fish extending dishes
- Uncooked food recipes (including some ingredients commonly cooked)
- Appetisers for otherwise dull dishes

- Imaginative use of herbs and spices
- Unusual combinations of home grown foods
- Use of imperfect fruits and vegetables

Each recipe contains enough for four average people. We have not attempted to cater for the very young, the old or sick, though there is no reason why The Small Island Diet should not be adapted to their needs. On average, as we have seen, people in Britain over-eat, but this does not mean that there aren't many who eat about the right amount, and for them our advice is simply to check the quality and balance of their diet. Neither does it mean there are not many who do not eat enough. To those who do so from choice, our advice is simple: eat more. To those whose budgets are inadequate we humbly urge them to concentrate on foods offering the best nutritional value for money – and *somehow* try to grow at least their own vegetables.

In these pages you will not find many 'luxury' recipes, even though we advocate feast days for special occasions. We know that on such days you will be using your own special recipes, with or without altering them.

We have used ounces and pints and Fahrenheit throughout, not only because they seem right for a book on food for Britain, but because we cook by them and we are pretty sure you do too – and will continue to do so for a long while. You will find a conversion table opposite with the numbers rounded off to suit the fairly imprecise needs of cookery. We do advise you to read a recipe through to the end before beginning to make it, chiefly to ensure that you have the right utensils and containers. We have not listed them separately because we wanted to save space.

All through, we stress the value of herbs and spices, not least because of the novelty and range of their flavours – from subtle hints to powerful 'heat' – can make a transition to a low meat diet almost unnoticed. You will find a table listing their names and principal uses overleaf. You will notice that we usually specify that spices and pepper should be freshly ground. This is because the whole seeds keep fresher when whole. Once ground they begin to lose their aromatic delights. To grind spices you can either use a pepper mill kept for the purpose, or else a pestle and mortar.

Figure 11 Metric conversion table (approximate)

1 oz.	28½ grams	25 grams	¾ oz.
2 oz.	57 grams	50 grams	1¾ oz.
½ lb	225 grams	100 grams	3½ oz.
1 lb	450 grams	225 grams	8 oz.
	(½ kilo)	450 grams	1 lb
¼ pint	140 millilitres	100 millilitres	1/5 pint
½ pint	285 millilitres	200 millilitres	1/3 pint
1 pint	570 millilitres	300 millilitres	½ pint
1¾ pint	1 litre	570 millilitres	1 pint
		1 litre	1¾ pints
Note: 1 pint = 20 fluid oz.			

We believe strongly that the plants of fields and hedgerows can play an important part in The Diet, and indeed we have included some of the commoner 'weeds' in the recipes. We advise everyone to explore this fascinating and valuable source of year-round nourishment, and to help we have suggested further reading in the Ideas for Action section.

You will notice that in only a few recipes do we specifically mention the pressure cooker. We have assumed that you're familiar with them and can decide when and how to use one if you wish. Because we have a solid fuel range, we use ours less than if we relied on gas or electricity. Also we don't find that the flavours and textures of vegetables pressure cooked compare with ordinary cooking. However, as you probably know, pressure cookers can offer big advantages: cooking time is about a third of normal, so you can save on fuel; tough meat quickly becomes tender; beans too cook fast; lastly you can cook a complete meal all at once and this can be extra useful if you have to rely on a camping stove during a power cut ... or indeed when camping!

We hope that the first recipe you try proves to be the first step on an adventurous journey which you will never regret. We wish you tranquil and rewarding cooking.

Figure 12 Essential Herbs and Spices
Here is a list of the herbs and spices used in our selection of recipes. There are many more than these, as any herb book will demonstrate, but they are the principal ones, and those which you should grow, pick or buy when you move over to The Small Island Diet. They are essential for variety and interest in your dishes, expecially when meat features less and less as the foundation of the meal. Those we have asterisked you can grow out of doors; Chives, Marjoram and the various kinds of Thyme can also be picked, for they grow wild. Buy spices whole, rather than ground, for they taste better and keep longer. In any case, buy in small quantities, for their shelf life is limited. You can dry your own herbs, of course, and, if you do, be sure to store them in dark jars with screw tops – malt and Marmite jars, for example.

Allspice	Dhania	*Mustard
*Basil	*Fennel	Nutmeg
*Bay leaves	Fenugreek	*Oregano
*Bergamot	Garam Masala	Paprika
*Borage	*Garlic	*Parsley
Caraway	Ginger	Pepper, white and black
Cardamon	*Horseradish	*Rosemary
*Chives	*Lemon Balm	*Sage
Cinnamon	*Marjoram	*Savory
Cloves	Methi	*Taragon
*Coriander	*Mint, various kinds	*Thyme, various kinds
Cummin	Mixed spice	Vanilla pods

5
SOUPS AND SALADS

A rich, full-bodied soup, made with meat or vegetable stock, and served with good bread can make a complete meal. Or a more delicate one may be an enticing introduction to good things to come. With imagination you can create 365 different soups a year, and if half of them are based on left-overs, then that's a justification for pride and not a source of guilt!

A blender can be your best friend, both for disguising left-overs, and for making soups from scratch. So much faster than using a sieve. Here we make a few suggestions for soups made with a blender, but you'll find plenty more in any of the specialised recipe books.

If you've been used to reaching for a tin, *please* save any stock of tins which you may have, strictly for real emergencies from now on. You'll know why we are so emphatic by now: over-priced; a waste of precious metal; resin linings can cause allergies; may contain additives; heavy on salt maybe; and probably contain hidden sugar.

Artichoke Soup

One more argument for growing your own vegetables is this economical and quickly made soup, so welcome on winter days.

1 lb Jerusalem artichokes
1 medium onion
1 stick celery
1 pint stock
½ pint milk
1 tablespoonful flour
Some butter or margarine
Chopped parsley
Salt and pepper
Vinegar

Scrub artichokes, scrape them and drop into water with 1 tablespoonful vinegar to keep their colour. Drain, cut up into small pieces. Finely cut up onion and celery. Melt a little butter or margarine in a strong pan and cook vegetables for a few minutes, stirring with wooden fork to prevent sticking. Add half the stock and cook until vegetables are quite tender – the smaller you cut them up the quicker they will cook – about 10 minutes. Pass through a sieve, then return to pan. Mix flour with some of remaining stock, add to pan with rest of stock and cook for about 3 minutes, stirring all the time. Finally heat milk, and combine with rest of ingredients. Serve immediately, garnished with chopped parsley.

Barley Vegetable Soup

A thick winter soup full of flavours and nourishment for which the vegetables need not be perfect.

1 teacupful pearl barley
2½ cupfuls of water
1½ pints rich meat stock, vegetable stock (page 236) or water
A collander full of mixed root vegetables other than potato and beetroot
1 large onion
1 large leek or the green pieces saved from other leek dishes
2 teaspoonsful mixed dried herbs
1 oz. butter
Yeast extract (if no stock)
Pepper and salt

Leave barley standing overnight in some cold water. Drain and cook in a pint-sized pan in 2½ cupfuls of boiling water. If you have no stock add 2 teaspoonsful yeast extract and mix in well. Simmer until tender – about 30 minutes – by which time the barley will have absorbed the water. Wash and scrub all root vegetables, leaving skins on if fresh from the garden or in good condition. Cut into small even pieces. Peel onion and cut into small pieces. Prepare leek, making sure there is no soil lurking in the folds. Cut into small chunks. In a large pan, melt fat, add all prepared vegetables. Toss and stir frequently to brown lightly – about 10 minutes. Add barley mixture, half the herbs and stock or water. Simmer for another 20 minutes, add rest of herbs 5 minutes before serving.

Celeriac Soup

This soup is just one way of using this remarkably accommodating, easily grown vegetable.

2 medium celeriac roots
1 large potato
½-¾ pint milk
¼ pint stock or water
1 oz. butter
Pepper and salt

Wash and scrub celeriac root very well. Coarsely grate. Peel and cut up scrubbed potato into small pieces. Melt butter in strong pan, toss celeriac and potato for a few minutes, taking care, as they tend to burn easily. Add stock or water and cook for about 10 minutes, stirring occasionally. Finally combine hot milk and seasonings. Serve at once. Decorate with finely chopped green celeriac tops. These can be stirred into soup at the last minute if preferred.

People who have over-indulged in fatty foods can help to clear their bloodstreams of accumulated fat simply by eating raw garlic. It lowers cholesterol levels too.

Chestnut Soup

This delicious nut, which grows in Britain, can be used for sweet or savoury dishes – just make sure you don't use 'conkers' by mistake! Here is the nut in a soup which is rich, filling and unusual. You'll really appreciate it in winter.

1 lb prepared chestnuts (page 189)
1 medium carrot
1 medium onion
3 sticks celery
1 tablespoonful oil
2 pints rich stock
2 tablespoonsful chopped parsley
1 clove
¼ pint cream or top of milk
Pepper and salt

Prepare and coarsely chop vegetables. In a large heavy pan cook vegetables in oil, stirring frequently until nicely browned. Chop chestnuts into small pieces and add to vegetables with stock, parsley and clove. Cover and simmer 30-45 minutes until chestnuts are soft. Pass through a sieve. Season and bring back to boiling point. Take off heat and add cream. Serve at once.

Gazpacho

This is our version of the famous Spanish cold soup. It's easy to make, colourful and refreshing on a warm summer's day, even better served with hot herb bread and cottage cheese. Never mind that it is 'foreign'; all the ingredients grow in Britain, and our recipe contains no oil.

1 lb ripe tomatoes or 1 x 2 lb jar bottled
½ lb firm tomatoes
4 fresh spring onions
1 or 2 cloves garlic
1 medium cucumber
1 medium green pepper
1 tablespoonful brown sugar
1 teaspoonful chopped fresh rosemary
½ teaspoonful chopped marjoram
Large bunch parsley
2 tablespoonsful wine
Little paprika
Some watercress
Salt and pepper
Ice cubes

Use only a stainless steel knife for this recipe.
Skin the ½ lb firm tomatoes in usual way. Take out seeds and pulp, save rest for later.
Cut up the 1lb ripe tomatoes and together with pulp from the ½ lb cook in wine for a few minutes until soft. Press through a sieve and cool. If using bottled tomatoes, just press through sieve. Cut cucumber in two (reserving one half for later.) Skin, take out any seeds, then chop. Cut green pepper in two (saving other half for later.) Take out seeds and white membrane

then chop. Prepare and chop garlic. Prepare spring onions, saving some of the firm green tops. Chop half, and save remaining for garnish. Put half tomato purée in blender with prepared vegetables, paprika, salt and pepper, and run for 1 minute until well blended and thick. Pour into large bowl. Add rest of tomato purée, sugar, wine (if not already used to cook tomatoes) and finely chopped marjoram and rosemary.
Stir well to combine.
combine.
Cut the reserved tomatoes and green pepper into small cubes. Leave some of skin on the reserved piece of cucumber, but take out seeds and pulp. Cut into small cubes. Thinly slice two remaining spring onions and fold all gently into the soup. Adjust seasoning to taste. Cover and chill in fridge or cold place until ready to use. Just before serving, chop parsley very fine. Divide soup into separate bowls. Drop a small ice cube into each and sprinkle with a generous spoonful of parsley on top. Decorate with a sprig of watercress.

Chilled Cucumber Soup

Cold, piquant soups make refreshing appetizers for hot summer days, and few can rival raw cucumber. This easy-to-grow vegetable ripens when the days are hottest, and today's varieties have the 'burp' bred out.

1 large, fresh cucumber
¾ pint milk
Small onion or spring onion
Some fresh rosemary
Little cream
2 oz. tasty cheddar cheese
Pepper and salt to taste

If you bought your cucumber from a commercial grower it could be coated in wax, so for safety peel it completely. Otherwise, simply wipe it, then cut in half and peel one half. From any cucumber discard a good inch of the stalk end which can be bitter. Cut the peeled half into small pieces and put in a blender with the milk, finely chopped onion, rosemary, salt and pepper. Blend for one minute. Cut four thin slices from remaining cucumber and put to one side. Cut up the rest and add to the blender with the cheese, finely grated. Blend for another minute. If you are using an unpeeled cucumber, the soup will be a pretty green colour.

Chill for as long as possible and serve in separate bowls, adding to each a little cream and a cucumber slice. If you like, decorate with tiny sprigs of mint and a few borage flowers.

Leek Soup

If you grow your own vegetables, you will know that leeks are among the easiest. And since you can pick them fresh from winter to early spring, they are a constant stand-by, such as a nourishing soup for lunch on cold days. After such a warming start, bread, cheese and chutney go down well. Or you can add finely grated tasty cheese to the soup and serve with hot bread or rolls.

4 leeks
2 medium potatoes
1 oz. butter
½ to ¾ pint milk
¼ pint hot water or chicken stock (page 236)
Salt
Freshly ground white pepper

Trim leeks and wash very well. Use all the white with a little of the green part only. (You can wash the rest of the green part well and use the outer leaves in the stockpot, inner ones for vegetable soup. They will keep for a few days in a plastic bag in the refrigerator). Cut leeks finely then cook in half of the butter until still crisp but not brown. Keep tossing and stirring with a wooden fork for about 5 minutes.

Scrub potatoes, peel and cut up into small chunks. (Peelings go into stockpot). Cook in another pan in ¼ pint of water or stock for up to 10 minutes, watching carefully that the chunks do not stick. When cooked add hot milk, seasoning and leeks and rest of butter. Adjust seasoning to taste.

Lettuce Soup

So long as you have a blender you can make this excellent hot or cold soup. Especially useful when lettuces are over-plentiful and need disguising if they are to be eaten willingly.

1 good sized head of lettuce or plenty of good quality outside leaves. Lettuce running to seed could be slightly bitter.
½ pint chicken stock (page 236)
or mild vegetable stock
½ pint milk
1 tablespoonful finely chopped parsley
1 tablespoonful finely cut chives
Very small piece of garlic
Salt and pepper to taste

Wash lettuce and discard white stem. Break into small pieces, put in pan with stock and cook for about 5 minutes until soft. Allow to cool. Put ¼ pint of milk, garlic, cooked lettuce and stock into blender. Run until well blended, about a minute. Return to pan, add rest of milk and chopped chives and re-heat but do not boil. Season to taste. Serve with croutons (page 93) and chopped parsley as garnish. Delicious served chilled.

Nettle Soup

This full-bodied soup is a good way to introduce the family to the idea of 'food for free'. Pick your nettles when they are young – wear gloves!

1 pint fresh nettle tops (Pick nettles and press into pint jug – you'll need plenty)
1 medium chopped onion
1 pint vegetable (page 236) or meat stock
½ pint milk
1 oz. butter
2 tablespoonsful sievings from wholemeal flour, oatmeal or left-over porridge
Salt and very little pepper

Wash nettles well in plenty of water and shake off excess water. Melt butter in strong pan and cook onions until soft. Add nettles and half stock, and cook for 10 minutes or until nettles are soft. Press through sieve, return to pan with rest of stock and sievings etc. (If using porridge, be sure to blend in evenly). Cook for further 10 minutes. Add hot milk to pan and mix well, but do not boil. Season to taste and serve with croutons (page 93).

Optional variations:
Just before serving fold in a well-beaten egg.
Or 4 rashers of streaky bacon cut into thin pieces and tossed in frypan to crisp. Or both!

Parsley Soup

Although parsley is probably our best known herb, convention dictates that it be almost exclusively confined to a sauce for fish or a derisive sprig for decoration. Yet parsley is rich in goodness – especially iron and vitamin A – and since you can buy or grow it all year round, it deserves a better deal. As a start make this easy soup – heartwarmingly hot in winter or refreshingly cool in summer.

Large bunch of parsley
3 tablespoonsful leftover creamed potatoes
¾ pint milk
1 small onion or 3 spring onions
1 oz. butter
1 teaspoonful salt
Pepper to taste

Wash parsley well and shake off excess water, then chop it finely, stalks and all. Put into blender the potatoes, half the milk, chopped onion, salt, pepper, parsley stalks chopped up with some of the tops, and blend for ½ minute. Heat rest of milk in pan and pour in the blender mixture, stirring all the time over moderate heat. Simmer for a few minutes but don't let it boil fiercely. Just before serving add the butter and fold in rest of finely chopped parsley tops.

If you have no blender, chop onion finely and cook in pan with a little of the milk until soft – a few minutes. Add the potatoes and work in the rest of the milk slowly until well mixed. Chop all the parsley very fine and add to the mixture. Fold in butter just before serving.

Extra tempting served with garlic croutons (page 93).

Puffball Soup

If you live near woods and fields you may find this unmistakeable large, round fungus (Latin name, *Lycoperdon giganteum*) under hedges or other cover. Up to a foot across, it is white when young, changing from yellow to green with age. It is perhaps the tastiest of all fungi and superb in soup. Don't be afraid to try this simple soup recipe.

½ lb young puffball
1 small onion or two spring onions with some of green part
½ pint milk
½ pint vegetable or chicken stock (page 236)
1 tablespoonful flour
½ oz. butter
Chopped parsley
Salt and white pepper

Wash off sand or soil from puffball. Take off leathery skin if you like but no need to, cut out any undesirable parts. Cut in ½ inch slices then into ½ inch cubes. Put in pan with stock and cook gently until tender – about 15 minutes. Cut the prepared onion up very finely and add to cooked puffball. Mix some of the milk with the flour and add to pan. Cook for a few minutes to thicken then add rest of milk heated, pepper and salt to taste. Add butter and stir until combined. Divide into individual dishes and garnish generously with parsley.

Optional variation:
If you prefer a creamed soup, put half the quantity in blender, blend for ½ minute then blend other half. Reheat, serve as before.

Pumpkin Soup

Pumpkin soup is so good it is surely surprising that it does not turn up more often, especially since pumpkin can be stored well into spring. You can make it with either fresh or left-over pumpkin and potato.

½ pint cooked puréed pumpkin
½ pint chicken or vegetable stock (page 236)
2 tablespoonsful mashed
or creamed cooked potato
¼ pint milk
1 tablespoonful chopped parsley
1 tablespoonful chopped chives
Little butter
Salt and pepper

Work potato and pumpkin together with some stock until smooth. Add chopped chives, rest of stock, pepper and salt to taste, and bring to the boil. Take off heat, add hot milk and butter, stirring until combined. Divide between four. Garnish with parsley.

In Britain now, one man in three is likely to suffer a heart attack or stroke before retirement, and among women the rate is increasing. Hence heart transplants – at around £25,000 a time – plus intensive care units and costly drugs. Prevention may be less glamorous, but it is cheaper and more effective... and, in the form of The Small Island Diet, thoroughly enjoyable.

Tomato Soup

Perhaps the most popular of all soups, this version tastes the way people have come to prefer. It will help take care of any glut and make use of less-than-perfect tomatoes.

*1½ lb ripe tomatoes (damaged ones will do)
or 2 lb jar of bottled tomatoes
1 medium onion
¾ pint of stock or milk or a mixture of both
(½ pint only if using bottled tomatoes)
2 oz. white or 81% flour
½ oz. butter
Bayleaf
Sprig rosemary
1 tablespoonful chopped parsley
Pepper and salt*

Wash and cut up tomatoes and chop prepared onion. Cook in some of stock with bayleaf and rosemary for 10 minutes. If using bottled tomatoes, pour some of juice into pan and cook onions only in it. Press onion and tomato mixture through sieve. Mix flour with a little of stock, put all stock and sieved mixture back into pan and cook for 3 minutes. Season to taste and stir in butter. If you use any milk at all it should be heated to boiling point and added slowly at the end of cooking to avoid curdling. Sprinkle parsley on top just before serving – with croutons if you like (page 93)

Watercress Soup

This natural source of iron makes one of the best of soups. Since none is over-cooked and half is uncooked, you get the benefit of vitamins with which it abounds. Serve hot or chilled.

2 large bunches of watercress
1 onion
½ oz. butter
2 tablespoonsful 81% flour
or cold sieved potato
¼ pint chicken stock (page 236)
1 pint milk
Salt and pepper

Cut off lower half inch of stalk from watercress. Wash the bunches carefully. Toss in collander to drain. Chop roughly half the cress and, with the finely chopped onion, simmer until soft in stock. Put cooked cress with half milk into blender for ½ minute or more, pour back into pan. Blend flour with a little of the milk and add to pan. If using potato stir in at this point. Put rest of milk into blender with uncooked watercress, blend for 1 minute. Cook contents of pan until thick, take off heat and stir uncooked watercress mixture slowly into pan, add butter, bring slowly back to just under boiling point. Test the seasoning. Serve at once with plain or garlic croutons (page 93).

Always cook more potatoes and root vegetables than you will need right away. They make quick soups or vegetable salads. They can also be made into a tasty dish by adding grated cheese and any left-over white sauce.

Croûtons for Soup and Salads

Plain:
The usual way to make croûtons is deep frying, but you can avoid such excessive fat intake. Simply cut four slices of bread about ½ inch thick, lightly butter then place on a baking sheet before cutting into squares. Bake in a slow oven at 300°F until crisp – time will depend on how new the bread is. Alternatively put under a slow grill as for toast, being careful not to burn them.

Garlic flavoured:
Crush a small clove of garlic into 2 oz. of butter, work it in very well and spread on the slices of bread. Cook as for plain croûtons. If there is any garlic butter left over, keep in a covered container for another time.

Croûtons can be made when the oven is on for other cooking and stored for later use, to be re-heated.

The Infinite Salad

A real salad is *an adventure* – you never know what you might find... and we're not talking about caterpillars! All year round there are British-grown vegetables and wild plants in plenty for nourishing and exciting concoctions. Herbs and dressings help to make any salad – some would say the dressing *is* the salad. It can certainly help to turn unlikely ingredients into a talking point – even left-over vegetables, for they don't *have* to be turned into soups or fry-ups. One word of warning, however: dressings and mayonnaises tend to be rich. They needn't be, especially if you make your dressings with yogurt.

In Britain we do not eat enough salads. Why? Because the same few vegetables keep turning up and we are not tempted; because out of season these obligatory few are expensive, imported or grown, heated under glass; and because as children we are not encouraged early enough. We need to get the salad habit – one a day at least, all year round, for health *and* enjoyment.

How to Make a Tossed Green Salad

Limp lettuce, pale peeled cucumber and watercress – if you're lucky – green salads in Britain are usually about as exciting as their soggy, over-cooked, hot vegetable counterpart!

A salad should be crisp and colourful with different shades of green, and the flavours should vary from one day to the next. Here are a few hints to achieve maximum nourishment and flavour.

Pick or cut your ingredients as close to eating time as possible. The fresher the salad, the crisper and more nourishing it is, for losses begin as soon as the ingredients are picked or severed from the growing plant.

If you have to buy the salad greens from a shop, discard outer leaves, wash in several waters, then dry immediately by whirling in a salad basket, a towel or pillowcase. Pop in a plastic bag and chill in the fridge. Then tear your salad greens into bite-sized pieces, lay them in a large wooden bowl, and, before adding a dressing, toss them with two wooden forks to mix everything up and diffuse all the different flavours. Always add the dressing at the table, just before serving.

Mixed Green Garden Salad

There's no need to keep to formal 'recipes' when putting a salad together. Be adventurous. Walk round the garden with scissors and a bowl and fill it, not with your conventional lettuce and so on, but with all sorts of little pieces of this and that.

From the vegetable patch cut off young sugar peas, beans, curly greens, sprouting broccoli, cabbage and brussels sprouts; the tops of onions, young beetroots and celeriac; celery, young spinach and swiss chard.

From the herb garden snip borage leaves, parsley, chives, mint and lemon balm.

And from inside or outside the garden, young hawthorn leaves, and 'weeds' such as young dandelions, chicory, shepherd's purse, land cress, ramsons – they taste of garlic – and young chickweed.

Don't expect to find everything ready for picking at any one time of the year.

Wash and dry your harvest. Cut or break the larger leaves into small pieces and put in a large salad bowl. For a little colour you could grate a young carrot. Toss all together, add a favourite oil and vinegar dressing, toss again. Or serve 'natural' with different dressings on the side. Decorate with borage flowers.

Until the neolithic revolution, about 10,000 B.C., when man first grew plants and tamed animals, he influenced the outside world no more than any other mammal. From then he diverged, consistently taking more from the world than he gave, changing the face of the earth and virtually all other life. The divergence and taking continue exponentially.

Variations on Raw Beetroot Salad

Most people only taste beetroot cooked and supersaturated in vinegar. This may be all right, but to appreciate its sweet succulence try it grated raw instead. You'll welcome it most in winter when salads are hardest to concoct. It makes an admirable complement to jacket-baked potatoes, whether 'natural', stuffed (see page 137) or sprinkled with grated cheese; to cold meats or simply to wholemeal bread and cheese.

1 medium beetroot
2 inches white part of leek
1 medium tart apple if available
Oil and vinegar dressing (page 108)
Freshly ground pepper

Optional variations:
Small onion
Celeriac
Horseradish
Celery
Parsley
Cooked Mayonnaise *(page 106)*
Garlic Dressing *(page 107)*

Scrub beetroot well then dry. Wash leek thoroughly to remove all sand. Grate beetroot. Slice leek. Grate apple. Put all in large mixing bowl and mix very well with fingertips or two forks until all leek is broken up evenly. Add dressing and pepper to taste. Toss until evenly distributed.

Ring the changes as often as you can. Instead of dressing use mayonnaise; or substitute onion for leek; or add ½ a grated celeriac or two good sized celery sticks cut up finely; or for an ultra simple version, just enjoy beetroot, onion and plenty of fresh parsley, with or without any dressing.

Whichever variation you choose, transfer it to a serving dish and decorate to add contrasting colour – with apple slices, cress or watercress for example.

Carrot, Apple and Sprouted Wheat Salad

Rich in vitamins A and C, especially invaluable – and welcome – in winter.

2 medium apples
2 medium carrots
1 teacupful sprouted wheat (page 234)
2 oz. sultanas or currants
Basic oil and vinegar dressing (page 108)

Wash apples, core and grate coarsely. Scrub carrots and grate coarsely. Put in large bowl and add sprouted wheat and sultanas. Pour over some oil and vinegar dressing to taste and toss with two forks. Serve at once.

Optional variation:
Use yogurt as a dressing if preferred.

Pickled Cucumber Salad

If you already have your own recipe for pickled cucumber, here's a touch of piquancy which you'll appreciate in winter or whenever salad greens are scarce. Use it to complement curries too.

Put some yogurt in a bowl and mix in a little of the vinegar from pickled cucumbers.
Add cucumber slices, 1 tablespoonful of finely chopped mint and, if you like, a little sugar or honey.

Dried Haricot Bean Salad

A basic recipe to which you can add cubed cold meat, cubed tasty cheese or chopped hard boiled egg. Useful in winter.

*½ lb dried haricot beans
1 medium onion
Some parsley
Oil and vinegar dressing (page 108)
1 garlic clove
Salt and pepper*

Cook beans until tender but not mushy, then drain well. Add dressing and add crushed clove of garlic while still hot. Add finely chopped raw onion, and parsley, salt and pepper to taste. Chill overnight.

Brussels Sprouts and Celeriac Salad

Both these vegetables can be enjoyed raw to make an unusual and refreshing salad at a time of the year when economical salad vegetables are otherwise costly and hard to find. No need at all for perfect specimens.

*Equal quantities sprouts and celeriac
A few raisins
Some yogurt (page 244)
Salt and pepper*

Trim and wash sprouts and shred very finely with sharp knife. Scrub, then peel celeriac and grate. Mix both vegetables thoroughly in large bowl with the fingers. Use enough yogurt to moisten salad well. Add salt and pepper to taste, and garnish with a few raisins.

Cucumber Raita

A highly refreshing adjunct for curries and other savouries which are enhanced by its cooling influence. Or for salad table.

1 large cucumber
1 pint yogurt
1 small onion (red if possible)
or 3 spring onions
¼ teaspoonful cayenne
Good pinch ground cinnamon
Little ground cloves
½ teaspoonful salt

Peel cucumber, leaving some of green showing, slice very thinly. Chop spring onion finely and some of green tops too, or grate an onion. Beat the onion, salt and spices into yogurt. Fold in cucumber. Place in serving dish and chill.

English Salad

A hearty, substantial, one-dish meal.

1 lb cooked salad or waxy potatoes
1 lb tomatoes
½ lb cooked green beans
Some lean cooked ham if liked

Cut up potatoes. Skin and seed tomatoes and cut into strips. Cut beans into inch pieces. Toss all together with uncooked mayonnaise (page 105). Leave for a few hours, then fold in some chopped ham. Serve with a tossed green salad.

Fish Salad

All sorts of ingredients come together in this appetising salad which makes half a pound of fish into a meal for four people.

½ lb cooked cold firm white fish
1 large crisp green pepper
2 large firm ripe tomatoes
1 large cupful cooked cold wholemeal macaroni
1 tablespoonful finely grated fresh horseradish
4 tablespoonsful mayonnaise (page 105 or 106)
Some salad pieces – lettuce, watercress, radish and so on

Cook macaroni in usual way so that it is firm, not mushy. Drain and transfer to large bowl – reserving water for stock. When cold, add 1 tablespoonful mayonnaise, folding into macaroni carefully to separate it. Meanwhile flake fish and cut pepper in half. Take out seeds and white membrane. Cut into small squares and add to macaroni. Cut tomatoes in two, take out seeds and pulp and dry. Cut into small squares and set aside. Add 3 more tablespoonsful mayonnaise to macaroni, together with flaked fish and, lastly, tomato. Toss with two forks very carefully to mix well, making sure fish does not go into a mush. Place on a bed of lettuce on a serving dish or in individual bowls. Decorate attractively with watercress, tomato rings, cucumber – or whatever you fancy.

Potato Salad

Can there be a more versatile vegetable than the potato? Here it is again in a salad suggestion you can serve all year round.

1 lb cooked diced new potatoes or a variety of old potatoes which don't 'fall'
– Desiré for example
1 small onion or 1 tablespoonful chopped chives
Mint, thyme, rosemary and parsley
2 hard boiled eggs
Black pepper
¼ pint or more cooked mayonnaise (page 106)

Slice one hard boiled egg, chop the other one and set both aside. While potatoes are still warm, combine in large bowl with finely chopped onions and a generous mixture of the herbs. Cover and let stand until quite cold. Add chopped egg and mayonnaise and combine together thoroughly. Pile onto a bed of crisp lettuce in a serving dish and decorate with the slices of egg.

Britain covers an area of just over 52 million acres – one for each of us, though only 45 million acres are fit to grow food. Of this, about 17 million acres can grow grass and crops in rotation. Another 12 million are permanent grass and the rest is rough grazing.

Tomato Jelly Salad

Bottled or imperfect ingredients are no bar to creating this unusual and eye-catching salad. Its spiciness is even more appreciated in winter months. Striking enough for a special occasion.

*2½ cups tomato purée
or imperfect tomatoes
2 flat tablespoonsful gelatine
1 small onion
1 small bay leaf
9 peppercorns
3 cloves
1 teaspoonful sugar
1 teaspoonful celery salt
4 tablespoonsful cold water
1 hard boiled egg
Some cottage cheese*

Soak gelatine in the water. Chop onion and cook in tomato, peppercorns, cloves and bayleaf until tender. Put through a sieve to discard cloves and so on. Stir in gelatine. Pour into small moulds to set. Unmould onto a bed of lettuce or watercress on individual plates, and decorate with cottage cheese, hard boiled egg, cold mixed vegetables and pieces of fruit. Serve a favourite dressing or mayonnaise on the side.

Bulgur Wheat Salad

The specially prepared wheat not only imparts a distinctive flavour and texture, but balances the salad to make it into a nourishing light meal on its own, if desired.

1 cupful bulgur (page 232)
3 large tomatoes
½ cupful chopped spring onions or chives
Plenty of chopped parsley
Oil and vinegar dressing (page 108)
or natural yogurt (page 244)
3 cupsful hot water

Soak bulgur for about 45 minutes in hot water, then drain very thoroughly through a sieve. Cut tomatoes in two, remove pulp and seeds and save for another dish. Cut up tomatoes into small chunks. Put bulgur, onions, chives and parsley into large bowl and mix, adding dressing. Lastly, just before serving, add tomatoes. Place on a bed of lettuce and decorate with, say, watercress to look inviting.

The Rich North, with less than a third of the world's people, takes about half the world's growth of cereals and feeds, 70 per cent of its share to livestock. The Poor South, with most of the people, eats 90 per cent of its share direct and feeds only 10 per cent to livestock.

Quick Mayonnaise

If you have a blender you can make this mayonnaise in a few minutes.

2 eggs (would suggest just yolks)
4 tablespoonsful cider vinegar
¼ pint oil
1 teaspoonful dry mustard
½ teaspoonful salt

Put all the ingredients with half the oil in blender and run for 1 minute or until thick. Add rest of oil a little at a time through hole in top of blender lid, keeping it running. Store in a cool place or refrigerator and it will keep a week.

Optional variation:
2 teaspoonsful sugar
Some chopped chives
Onion
Mixed herbs and so on

Cooked Mayonnaise

If you prefer a less oily mayonnaise, try this one. Store it in a cool place and it should keep for a month. Good for coleslaw.

*1 egg
2 teaspoonsful sugar
4 tablespoonsful milk
4 tablespoonsful cider vinegar
1 teaspoonful dry mustard
1 oz. butter or margarine
Pepper and salt*

Melt butter in pan over low heat taking care not to heat it. Add mustard and mix to smooth paste. Combine eggs and sugar in bowl and beat well. Stir in milk. Add vinegar very slowly, stirring all the time, but don't worry if it goes thick. Pour onto butter and mustard mixture a little at a time to mix evenly. Cook over low heat, stirring all the time until thick, taking care not to let it boil.

When making coleslaw try getting away from white cabbage and use savoy instead, which is much sweeter and tastier. Coleslaw will be more appealing and digestible if cut finely – to children especially.

Garlic Dressing

Transforms even a mundane salad – unless you have the misfortune not to appreciate garlic. Even so, why not have a try?

2 cloves garlic
1 egg yolk
1 cupful oil
3 tablespoonsful cider or wine vinegar
½ teaspoonful dry mustard
1 teaspoonful salt

Crush garlic. Make a paste with garlic, salt, mustard, egg yolk and 1 tablespoonful vinegar dribbled in slowly. Beating all the time, add ½ the oil, then the rest of the vinegar slowly while still beating, and finally rest of oil – again slowly and still beating gently after each addition. Store covered in a cool place.

Goats and sheep were the first animals to be tamed by man for food, probably around 9000 B.C. Pigs were next, about 7000 B.C. and cattle a thousand or so year later. Meat and the non-food by-products of hides, bristle, wool and so on, were the first incentives, but two unlooked-for benefits soon manifested: milk and muscle-power. All but the pig became agricultural labourers, to plough, to sow and thresh – man's first power tools.

Quick Oil and Vinegar Dressing

Use this 'first aid' to transform a repetitious collection of summer salad vegetables into an appetizing creation. Use it for gluts of lettuce or tomato especially, and when visitors arrive unexpectedly but strategically timed for lunch or supper.

Some cider vinegar
Some oil
2 teaspoonsful sugar or honey
Salt
Pepper
Dry mustard (1 teaspoonful, more if liked)
Optional variations:
Garlic
Fresh or dried herbs

Take a 12 oz. jam jar with a tight-fitting lid and fill it 1/3 full with vinegar. Add sugar, salt, mustard and a little pepper. Shake vigorously until evenly mixed. Add enough oil to leave ½ inch space at the top and again shake vigorously until thick. Pour into a serving jug or add directly to tossed salad.

For variety try crushing a piece of garlic into it. You can add fresh or dried herbs, and substitute honey for sugar too. Use the same jar whenever you want this dressing – it saves messy washing up.

Yogurt Salad Dressing

For a dressing with a zesty sharpness, fold together half yoghurt and half cooked mayonnaise (page 106). For added flavouring use chopped chives, grated onion, garlic, various herbs and salt and pepper to taste. Always fold in the yogurt before adding any flavourings. To make your own yogurt see page 244.

6
MAINLY MAIN DISHES

Our recipes may not show it, but they have been carefully balanced so that they contain the nutrients we need in roughly the right proportions – though always with an eye to flavour and colour. We have not suggested any menus, but you will soon spot which recipes appeal to you as partners in any one meal.

You will find a few Indian, Chinese and Italian style dishes here because, as we explain, their ingredients – and often the way they are cooked – conform remarkably well to The Small Island Diet. They do not waste precious protein, for example, and we can learn from them. On an affluent diet we waste protein when we serve peas and beans, fresh or dried, with meat, just as we waste it if we eat a high protein meat meal more than once a day.

You will not find many luxury dishes – such as ones based on salmon, oysters or the game birds. It's not that we disapprove of eating them, any more than we would ban feast days. What you *will* find are enough recipes, all devoid of excessive richness, to stimulate you to experiment.

Vegetables – Heart and Soul of the Meal
When planning a meal most people's first thought is 'What meat?' followed by 'What veg?' As if they were second class food, vegetables tend to take second place – and too often the cooking of them *is* second rate. When vegetables start being cooked to perfection, however, meat gently slips into second place, sometimes to vanish almost unnoticed. When this happens, meals become better balanced, no less nutritious and delicious – and generally more economical.

Now there's no special magic to cooking perfect vegetables. The trouble is that most people cook them for much too long in too much water. Potatoes are an exception, but many vegetables need no added salt in cooking because they contain their own natural salts and minerals. When you cook them quickly with little or no water they retain their salts and minerals along with all their flavour and nourishment. Some vegetables release water when cooked; with others you may need to add a little once or twice; but when they turn out to be adequately cooked at the same time as the pan is all but dry, you've mastered the art. You have the satisfaction of knowing that you haven't thrown any taste or goodness out with the leftover water. Some vegetables do need water thoughout, but in that case you can save the water for stock.

Remember that the chief object in cooking is to burst the cellulose cells that hinder digestion of the starch they contain. Sometimes a little longer is needed to tenderise the cellulose, but beyond a certain point extra cooking simply destroys taste, colour and nourishment – especially vitamins – and wastes fuel.

You can cook all root vegetables (except potatoes) the 'minimum water' way, also cabbage, leeks, celery and frozen peas and beans. You can also cook sprouts and broccoli this way, but we find that the way described below encourages an even better texture. Fresh peas and beans also need this kind of treatment. Cook with this sort of 'tender loving care' and the improvement can be dramatic. All the same, don't forget that results can often be enhanced – and variety added – by sauces and herbs.

Tossed Carrots

Carrots double their flavour when cooked with minimal water – not that this is the *only* way to cook this excellent, ill-treated vegetable.

1 lb carrots
2 tablespoonsful water
Salt and pepper
A little butter

Scrub carrots and take out any marked places. Halve lengthwise and cut into pieces about ⅛ inch thick. Put water in pan and keep tossing the carrots with the lid on over medium heat. Watch carefully and when the water has gone the carrots should be crisp but cooked – about 5 minutes. Toss in a little butter. Salt and pepper to taste.

Crunchy Sprouts and Broccoli

Fully cooked and never soggy – all within eight minutes!

Sprouts or broccoli
Salt and pepper
Boiling water
Knob of butter

Trim sprouts and wash. If broccoli stalks are thick, cut lengthwise, so that they cook as quickly as the flowerets, and wash. (Never leave any green vegetables standing in salty water.) Have ready a pan of boiling water with a little salt dissolved. Add the vegetable and boil – sprouts for 5 minutes, broccoli for 8 – until tender and crunchy-crisp. Drain immediately and transfer to serving dish. Glaze with butter and add freshly ground pepper. Time everything for immediate eating.

Potato and Tomato Casserole

This will warm you from autumn to early spring. No meat is needed and the potatoes don't have to be perfect.

1½ lb potatoes
1 oz. butter, margarine or dripping
1 lb bottled or fresh tomatoes
1 teaspoonful mixed, dried herbs
Salt and pepper

Scrub potatoes and either peel or, if not too old, leave skins on. Cut into thin slices. Melt fat in a pan and toss potato slices in it to coat, then place in casserole. If using fresh tomatoes pop in boiling water for a few minutes and then in cold water. Take off skins. Add whole tomatoes to potatoes with salt, pepper and herbs, then cover. Cook on bottom shelf with other dishes in moderate oven until potatoes are soft – 45 minutes to 1 hour.

The Poor South country, Senegal, receives milk-powder aid from France. It also exports peanuts for animal feed. Because the peasants are denied the use of the land occupied by peanut plantations, they and their compatriots are poor and often hungry. In effect, French cows eating peanuts produce a milk surplus which is sent back to Senegal as milk powder as food aid which its people wouldn't need if the country didn't export peanuts for French cows!

Braised Red Cabbage

Few local vegetables are so slandered and ill-treated as the cabbage. Any variety of cabbage, properly cooked, is a delight: a red cabbage, however, braised with this blend of spices and other goodies will make any meat meal into a treat – pork especially. In the unlikely event of any being left over, you can enjoy it cold.

About 2 lb red cabbage
2 medium onions
4 big cooking apples
2 cloves garlic
2 oz. butter, oil or dripping
2 flat tablespoonsful brown sugar
1 cup red wine
1 cup water or vegetable stock (page 236)
2 tablespoonsful cider vinegar
¼ teaspoonful nutmeg
¼ teaspoonful allspice
¼ teaspoonful caraway seed if liked – or more spice
Salt and freshly ground black pepper

Remove hard core of cabbage, also any very tough ribs, and cut into about ½ inch slices. Cook in saucepan for about 5 minutes in butter, stirring a couple of times to make sure it doesn't stick, then take off heat. Cut onions into thin half moons. Core apples and cut into thick slices. Fill a casserole with successive layers of cabbage, onion and apple, starting with cabbage. Add a little crushed garlic, salt, pepper and spices to each layer. Lastly sprinkle with sugar. Mix together wine and water (or stock), then pour over and cook with lid on in moderate oven until cabbage is quite tender – about 1 to 1½ hours. Make sure it does not dry out. You can use a heavy-based pan instead if you prefer, simmering on top of the stove for about the same length of time.

Jerusalem Artichokes

For some people this root vegetable's nutty flavour is an acquired taste. It is worth acquiring, so don't be put off by its slightly grey appearance when cooked. If buying them, make sure the tubers are firm – reject if at all wrinkled or leathery. They are easy to grow, but if you do, reserve a corner for them, for they will reappear year after year and tend to spread. If you mulch them in autumn you will have no problem digging them up in late winter frosts. You can eat them raw, cut up finely, and dressed with oil and vinegar. Or lightly boiled for 10 to 15 minutes to tender crispness – don't over-cook them.

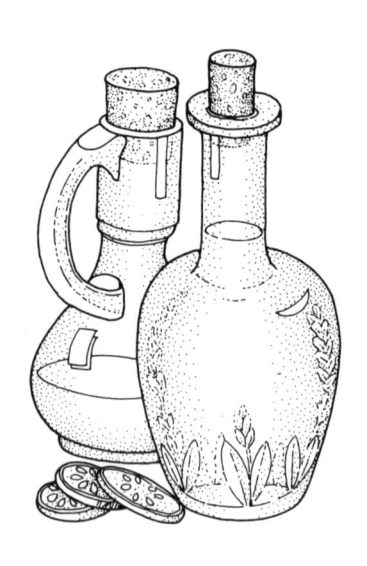

Jerusalem Artichokes with Sprouts

Served together, these two vegetables complement each other wonderfully – especially appreciated in winter's 'hungry gap'.

1½ lb artichokes
1 lb sprouts
½ pint white sauce (page 190)
Some nutmeg

Scrub and scrape artichokes and drop each one into cold water and vinegar to keep their colour. Prepare the sprouts. Pour boiling water into a pan with 1 tablespoonful vinegar and 1 teaspoonful salt. Cook artichokes until tender-crisp – no more than 15 minutes. While artichokes are cooking make sauce and add ¼ teaspoonful of freshly grated nutmeg, more if you like. Drain artichokes, put into serving dish and pour over sauce, keep warm. Cook sprouts for 3 minutes in the still boiling water in which you cooked artichokes. Time them from when water returns to boil. Drain into a collander, then pop back into a pan with a little melted butter or margarine to glaze, adding a little nutmeg while tossing. Decorate round the dish of artichokes with the glazed sprouts and serve immediately.

Savoury Sliced Pumpkin

This delicious, versatile vegetable is grossly underestimated in Britain. It can be embarrassingly prolific however, and though a good keeper it demands some imagination if the crop is to be eaten before deteriorating in storage. This recipe will make use of any pumpkins beginning to 'go' – or indeed perfect ones too.

Some pumpkin slices
2 medium onions
1 lb tomatoes
Wholemeal breadcrumbs
Some flour
Little butter and oil
Salt and pepper

Cut prepared pumpkin into ¼ inch slices and coat with flour. Put some oil in a heavy frypan and cook slices side by side until tender, turning once. Keeping cooked slices hot, continue until enough for several layers in your serving dish. Prepare onions and cut finely into half moon pieces. Put 1 tablespoonful oil in a pan, toss onion to coat with oil and cook for about 5 minutes until melted. Skin tomatoes, chop and add onions with some pepper and salt. Cook until tomatoes are tender and well mixed with onion – another 5 minutes or so. Arrange the pumpkin, tomato and onion mixture in layers on heated serving dish. Add a little melted butter to enough breadcrumbs to cover pumpkin mixture. Crisp under grill. Highly recommended with roast meat or chicken. Good as a light meal alone.

Optional variation:
For extra flavour, if desired, mix 1 teaspoonful mixed herbs with breadcrumbs or add garlic to onion and tomato mixture.

Pumpkin Surprise

No meat is needed to create this nourishing mid-winter boon of ingredients not usually cooked together. If you have a glut of pumpkins, you can be sure of several encores.

1½ lb of prepared, dark orange fleshed pumpkin
2 medium onions
½ pint plain white sauce (page 190)
¼ lb grated tasty cheese
4 eggs
4 tablespoonsful wholemeal breadcrumbs
2 oz. butter
2 teaspoonsful sage
Pepper and salt

Butter a 2 to 3 pint fireproof dish. Prepare pumpkin, cut into ½ inch cubes and steam or otherwise cook them until soft but not mushy. Should be dry when cooked. Mash, add pepper and salt to taste and keep hot. Cut up onion finely and cook in 1 oz. of butter until soft and golden. Keep hot. Make white sauce and add to the cooked, mashed pumpkin, mixing well. Grate cheese. Put half the pumpkin mixture in bottom of buttered dish and spread evenly with cooked onions. Break eggs carefully in 4 places on top of this. Sprinkle half the cheese on top of eggs and then on rest of pumpkin mixture. Mix rest of cheese with sage and breadcrumbs and sprinkle on top. Dot with butter. Bake in a moderate oven until top is nicely browned and crisp – 10 to 15 minutes.

Optional variation:
If you really fancy the idea of meat, substitute slices of boiled ham for the eggs.

Baked Shaggy Caps

Mushroom is only one of dozens of tasty edible fungi, and high on our list is the shaggy cap – also called lawyer's wig, inkhorn, inkytop and ink cap (Latin: *Coprinus comatus*). Common in fields, road verges and playing fields from June to November. Pick young while still firm and white. Eat while fresh. Here's how to cook them with minimal fat. Complete in themselves without meat.

Liberal quantity of shaggy caps
Some butter
Fresh brown breadcrumbs
Pepper and salt

Pull stalks from caps. Butter a pie dish and cover base with shaggy caps, breadcrumbs and salt and pepper to taste. Dot with butter. Continue with similar layers, finishing with a good layer of breadcrumbs. Dot with butter. Cook in a moderate oven at 350°F for about 1 hour by which time the breadcrumbs should be nice and crisp on top.

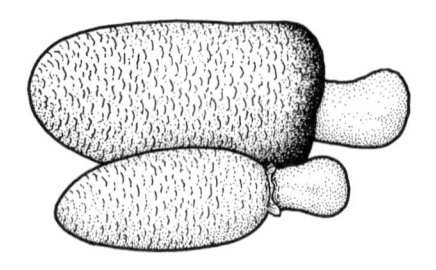

In Praise of Swedes

One historic British event of the mid-seventies was The Great Potato Famine. People by the million queued for them, fought for them, paid through the nose for them, stole them ... or went without. Yet swedes by the ton were refused, ignored and left to rot simply because people by the million didn't know how to cook them, or knew too well the almost tasteless soggy mush of badly cooked swedes.

Cooked properly, however, they are delicious. Each crisply tender cube of the golden vegetable is sweet and firm, with a distinctive rich and mellow flavour. You can eat them raw too. Coarsely grated in winter salads they add a welcome, robust 'bite' to them, as well as timely vitamin C.

Swedes are easy to grow and store. In southern counties, preferably mulched, you can leave them in the ground all winter. New garden varieties have been bred for flavour, and when really fresh they do not even need peeling.

Root crops in general, except for potatoes, carrots and parsnips, tend to be maligned and overlooked. Yet in Britain, where they grow so well, they are a valuable, staple food. They add much needed variety to our long winters – at least cost.

Every minute, 28 people die as a consequence of hunger – 21 of them children. More people have died as a result of hunger and malnutrition in the past five years than have been killed in all the wars, revolutions and murders in the past 150 years. Yet there is no food shortage!

Swedes Cooked to Perfection

Scrub the swedes – preferably not too large – and, if bought and no longer fresh, peel them. Cut into ¼ inch strips or ½ inch cubes – about 1½ lb for 4 people. Put a small amount of water in a large, strong pan, add swedes and cook over medium heat with lid on – no longer than 10 minutes, by which time the water should have gone. Shake every few minutes while cooking. When cooked, pieces should be crisp, firm and tender. Remove from heat and pour over some top of the milk or thin cream. Add freshly ground pepper and a little salt to taste, then toss over low heat to cover all the pieces. Serve at once.

Sauce for Summer Vegetables

All through this book we contend that indigenous vegetables – preferably grown organically – properly cooked and occasionally garnished are a dish on their own. Build the meal round them, and often as not, meat becomes superfluous. At no time is this truer than in summer, when nature virtually explodes in a continuing feast of fresh vegetables. Although they can be superb on their own, you may prefer them with a creamy sauce. Here is just one of many which will enhance potatoes, peas, carrots, broad and runner beans, young marrows and all summer greens. Not that you're likely to eat all these at once! We find that new potatoes covered with sauce, together with say, young carrots and freshly picked peas, are unsurpassed – even as a meal on their own.

¾ pint milk
1 tablespoonful white flour
½ oz. butter
3 or 4 spring onions
2 tablespoonsful chopped mixed herbs such as parsley, thyme and rosemary
1 egg
Salt and pepper

Melt butter in pan, add chopped spring onions (best green part as well) and 1 tablespoonful herbs. Cook until onion is soft – about 3 minutes. Take off heat, add some of the milk and work in the flour. Heat rest of milk and add a little at a time; cook for 5 minutes, stirring all the time until thick and flour is cooked. In the meantime boil egg for 4 minutes. Put in cold water and when cool enough to handle, shell and mash with a fork to break up the white into small pieces. (Please don't hard boil the egg because it spoils the sauce.) Fold egg and rest of herbs into the sauce, heat through but do not boil. Serve immediately.

Stuffed Aubergines

We can grow aubergines (or eggplant) in this country now. Here is one of our favourite ways to serve this luscious vegetable as a meat extender.

4 medium aubergines
(about 5 inches long is a good size)
2 medium onions
¾-1 lb minced best beef
1 lb ripe or 1lb jar bottled tomatoes
¼ lb mushrooms
¼ lb tasty Cheddar cheese
4 tablespoonsful oil
2 tablespoonsful chopped parsley
1 teaspoonful dried mint or 2 of fresh
Salt and pepper

Take off stems and cut eggplants lengthways. Scoop out with sharp spoon to leave shells ½ inch thick, then salt and pepper them. Chop prepared onion, and pieces of eggplant. Set aside. Skin tomatoes if necessary and · chop. Wash and slice mushrooms. Grate cheese. Heat oil in a heavy pan. *Sauté* onion and eggplant until nicely browned, stirring often – about 10 minutes. Remove from pan with slotted spoon and keep warm. Add minced beef to pan, break up with a wooden fork and cook, stirring all the time until nicely browned.
Add cooked eggplant and onion, parsley, mint, tomatoes and mushrooms to pan. Combine ingredients thoroughly and cook for about 5 more minutes.
Test the seasoning.
Place eggplant shells in oven-to-table dish. Fill with meat and vegetable mixture. Any leftover mixture can go round eggplant halves. Cover with tinfoil and cook in preheated 350°F oven for 30 minutes. Remove foil and sprinkle grated cheese evenly over eggplant halves. Return to oven (high shelf) for 10 minutes to crisp and brown cheese. Serve with a green salad (page 95) or cucumber raita (page 100).

Stuffed Cabbage

A tasty mid-winter meal which helps to make the meat go further.

1 Savoy cabbage about 7 inches across the tight centre
½ lb minced pork
2 medium sized cooking apples
1 large onion
Salt and pepper

Cut off large outside leaves of Savoy – wash them and use for stock. Place Savoy in a bowl of salted water for about 10 minutes to lure out any creepy crawlies, then shake off all water and drain well. With a sharp knife cut out centre of Savoy, leaving about an inch at the edge for a firm case. Finely shred what you have removed, discarding any thick ribs. Grate apples and slice onion. In a non-stick frypan stir-fry pork until lightly browned and cooked – about 10 minutes. Take pork out with a slotted spoon and set aside. If there is a lot of fat in the pan, drain some of it off. Put in shredded cabbage, onion and apple, stirring all the time, until soft – about 5 minutes. Add cooked pork and mix all together very well with juices in pan. Oil a large piece of foil – enough to make a parcel of the Savoy case and set it in the centre. Fill case with the pork mixture and wrap up tightly. Put boiling water in a baking dish, set the prepared Savoy on a rack over the water and bake in a 400°F oven for 30 to 45 minutes. Remove from oven, carefully lift onto a deep dish, fold back foil over top of dish, turning under to make a neat display for serving.

Savoury Cauliflower

Everyone knows cauliflower cheese, but here is a different way to make a feature of this versatile vegetable. Useful during late winter and early spring, appetising with or without meat, it combines some familiar ingredients in an unusual way.

1 medium cauliflower
¼ lb button mushrooms
3 eggs
3 tablespoonsful milk
Little butter
1 tablespoonful chopped parsley
2 teaspoonsful chopped chives
Pepper, salt to taste
Pan boiling salted water

Prepare cauliflower and break into inch flowerettes. Drop into boiling salted water for 2 minutes. Drain very well. Wash mushrooms and cut in two if necessary. Toss in a little butter, put lid on and cook for 5 minutes on low heat and then without lid a few minutes more to absorb juices. Beat eggs very well and add salt, pepper and milk. Stir to combine. Butter the dish very well. Put in a layer of cauliflower, then mushrooms with sprinkling of herbs until dish is full. Pour gently over beaten egg. Cook like a custard in dish of boiling water until set and golden – about 30 minutes in a moderate oven.
Serve with tomato and favourite green salad and baked potato or garlic bread.

Optional variation:
Chopped cooked ham in place of mushrooms.

Carrot and Potato Pancakes

Colourful and quickly made. Most appreciated in winter, or by children at any time for tea.

3 large grated carrots
3 medium grated potatoes
3 tablespoonsful finely chopped onion or leek
2 tablespoonsful finely chopped parsley
¼ pint milk
¼ lb flour
3 eggs
Freshly ground pepper
½ teaspoonful salt

Make a batter of eggs, flour and milk and combine thoroughly with all other ingredients. Have a little oil in a hot non-stick fry pan. Drop in mixture by tablespoonsful and cook until golden, turning once. Serve immediately.

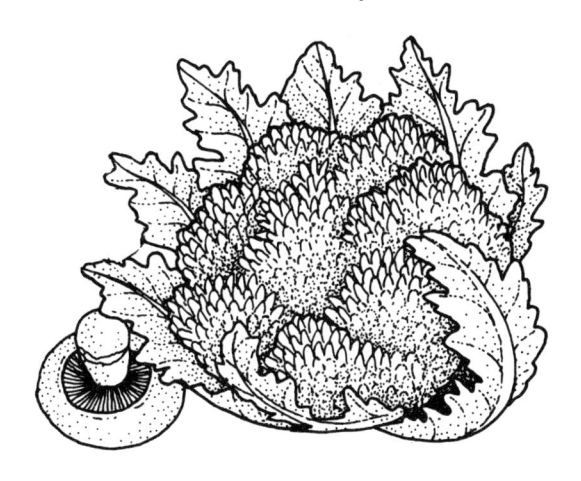

Celeriac Croquettes

This novel change from plain potatoes can be eaten in place of roast potatoes with meat, as an alternative topping to shepherd's pie, or – with grated cheese and a salad – as a meatless meal.

1 good sized celeriac
¾ lb pre-cooked mashed
or creamed potatoes
1 egg yolk
½ oz. butter
Little oil
Breadcrumbs
Pepper and salt

Scrub and clean celeriac well then coarsely grate. Melt butter in pan and sauté celeriac until soft but not burnt. Allow to go cold. Mix well with potato and egg yolk and leave in cool place for a few hours until quite firm, then form into rounds or 'fingers'. Dip in beaten egg white then breadcrumbs and fry in a little oil until golden and heated through.

Optional variation:
If you intend this mixture to be a topping for shepherd's pie, mix the cooked celeriac with the potato and egg and use while still hot.

Sweet Corn Bake

Piping hot, juicy sweet corn on the cob with a little butter, salt and ground pepper to taste, held in the hands or with forks if too hot! Is there any more mouthwatering way? In our fickle summers, however, cobs don't always fill out evenly. With this recipe no one need know yours are less than perfect. And even if they are, it makes a welcome change in the odd years of glut. Eat it as a main dish, or to supplement meat – especially bacon or pork – or to complement other vegetables such as stuffed cabbage (see page 123).

About 4 medium sized cobs
4 eggs
1 teaspoonful salt
4 oz. fresh wholemeal breadcrumbs
A little butter
Pepper to taste

With a sharp knife cut kernels from cobs on a plate to catch their juice. Beat eggs until frothy. Add kernels to eggs. Combine with salt and pepper to taste. Butter a 2 pint pie dish well. Pour in ingredients. Top with ½ inch of breadcrumbs dotted with butter. Bake in a 300°F oven for 1-1½ hours or until firm and golden.

Hot Sweet Corn

Here is another way of using imperfect sweet corn cobs, or an excess of perfect ones – a piquant dish which can be ready in a fraction of the time of Sweet Corn Bake.

4 to 6 cobs of sweet corn
1 oz. butter or 2 tablespoonsful corn oil
1 large onion
1 green pepper
4 tomatoes
3 tablespoonsful cream
Pepper and salt
A few dashes of tabasco

Cut raw corn kernels from the ears with a very sharp knife. Prepare and cut the onion into fine slices. Cut pepper into four. Discard white bits and seeds, then cut into strips. Skin and chop tomatoes. Heat butter or oil in medium sized pan. Put corn and onions and pepper in first and cook until corn is light golden brown and onion glazed, stirring all the time to avoid sticking – about 5 minutes. Add the tomato and cook for a further 5 minutes over gentle heat. Season with salt, pepper and tabasco. At the end of cooking stir in the cream just before serving. Eat right away with green side salad and hot bread for perfection.

Pork and Hot Sweet Corn

An appetising recipe to make a little pork go
a long way.

*½ to ¾ lb of fresh minced pork
or diced cold pork
Hot corn ingredients (see previous page)*

Cook the pork until golden in a little oil or butter, keeping it on the move to avoid sticking. Remove from the pan with a slotted spoon and keep hot.
Proceed as for Hot Corn, using the fats and juices to cook the vegetables. When these are cooked, pour off any remaining fat. Add a little stock or water if necessary and then the pork, salt, pepper,
tabasco and cream.
Serve immediately – do not let it boil.

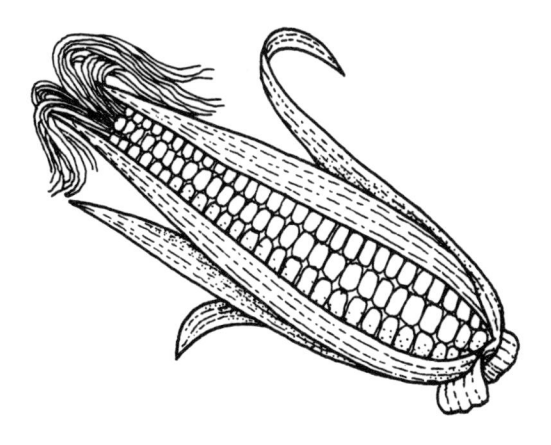

Baked Stuffed Cucumbers

'Cool as a cucumber,' we say, ignoring that cucumbers needn't be confined to salads but can be cooked like small marrows and eaten piping hot. Firmer and spicier than marrows, they are even better when stuffed with a filling which can include eggs, meat or fish to make these concentrated foods go further. This recipe will help take care of gluts, for cucumbers can 'go mad' in good seasons. We have grown buckets of ridged cucumbers (the outdoor variety), while just one female plant in an unheated greenhouse can feed a family of four all summer – with still more to give away!

4 to 6 cucumbers, depending on size
2 spring onions
4 eggs
½ pint seasoned white sauce (page 190)
Parsley
Breadcrumbs
A little butter

Hard boil and chop eggs. Wash and dry cucumbers, then cut in half lengthwise and scoop out seeds with sharp-edged spoon. Blanch in boiling water for 3 minutes, remove carefully and drain. Butter a shallow ovenproof serving dish and arrange the cucumbers close together. Chop onions and 2 tablespoonsful parsley finely. Combine your preferred ingredients to fill cucumbers with mixture. Sprinkle over with breadcrumbs, dot with butter and cook in a moderate oven for 20 minutes.

Optional variation:
Leftover chicken or fish for filling

Leek and Potato Pie

A little bacon goes a long way as its flavour permeates this savoury pie. Helps see you through winter to early spring and make use of imperfect potatoes. Very economical.

6 medium potatoes
4 leeks
¼ lb or more of streaky bacon
½ to ¾ pint hot milk
Little butter
2 tablespoonsful fresh sage
or 1 of dried
Salt and pepper

Scrub potatoes and peel, saving peeling for stock. Cut into thin slices, put in collander, wash under running tap and let drain. Prepare leeks, cutting in two, lengthways, to make sure there is no soil lurking in the leaves. Cut into inch pieces and set aside. Remove bacon rind with sharp knife and cut bacon into inch pieces. Well butter an oven-to-table casserole about 3 to 4 inches deep, then line with some of the potato slices, pressing them well onto the butter. Fill dish with potato slices, leek and bacon, a layer of each at a time, and sprinkling each layer with finely chopped or dried sage, salt and a little ground pepper. Finish with potato, making sure this last layer is placed close together to form a crust. Very carefully pour over the hot milk. Sprinkle top with salt and freshly ground pepper and dot with butter. Cook covered in a 250°F oven for 1½ hours. Remove lid for last ½ hour to brown the top.
Serve as a main dish with a green vegetable or salad.

Stuffed Marrow

This colourful dish fulfils in the eating all that it promises. Serve it either as a vegetarian dish or as a way of making meat go further.

4 slices from a good sized marrow, each a good inch thick
2 medium onions
1 lb tomatoes or 1 lb jar bottled tomatoes
1 medium carrot
Small piece cabbage – about ¼ lb
1 leek
1 teacup porridge oats
2 tablespoonsful oil
1 teaspoonful dried mint or 2 teaspoonsful fresh mint
1 tablespoonful chopped parsley
1 teaspoonful salt
Freshly ground black pepper to taste
½ pint thick cheese sauce (page 190)

Optional variations:
1 teacupful boiled wheat (page 231)
1 teacupful wholemeal breadcrumbs
Large clove garlic
½ lb minced cooked pork or beef

Wash and dry marrow, and with a large knife cut out 4 slices from its centre, a good inch thick. Take out seed and stringy pieces with a sharp knife or pastry cutter.

Have ready a large pan with about 1 inch of boiling water. Place marrow pieces in it side by side, on end. Cook for 5 minutes, then turn over and cook another 5 minutes. Carefully take out and drain in collander. Heat a tablespoonful oil in a large oven-to-table baking dish. Lay in it the marrow slices and turn once to coat in oil. Keep hot in the bottom of a moderate oven.

Chop onion finely, slice leek extra fine, grate carrot and shred cabbage. Chop any ends of marrow left after peeling, but no more than 2 tablespoonsful. Drain well the bottled tomatoes, or skin and chop the fresh ones. Heat 1 tablespoonful oil in large strong based pan. Add tomatoes and rest of vegetables and stir-fry with wooden fork until almost tender – about 5 minutes, then seasonings, herbs, oats or wheat. If you plan to use this recipe as a meat extender, leave out oats and the alternative, cooked wheat, and use 1 teacupful breadcrumbs and the minced meat, together with the crushed garlic if liked. Fill the marrow centres with mixture, pressing down firmly. Cook in moderate oven for 30 minutes. Remove from the oven and top each portion with cheese sauce. Pop back in oven until sauce is golden brown and bubbling. Serve from the baking dish decorated with bunches of parsley or watercress.

Bean Roast

This dish usually conjures up a vision of imported beans. It needn't. You can make even more tempting bean roasts with ones grown right here. Best of all are daffa beans, rich and nutty-tasting – the newer variety of the good old English field or tic bean, basis of traditional Brown Windsor soup. You can also use broad or runner beans which you've allowed to ripen in the pod – yet another way of coping with a glut. (Ripe runner beans taste like imported butter beans.)

*1 lb cooked sieved beans
(weighed after sieving)
2 medium onions
1 medium carrot
1 leek
4 skinned or 4 bottled tomatoes
1 teacupful porridge oats
1 egg
2 tablespoonsful oil
A little strong Cheddar cheese
1 clove garlic
1 tablespoonful fresh mixed chopped herbs
or 2 teaspoonsful dried
2 teaspoonsful salt
Freshly ground pepper*

*Optional variation:
Boiled wheat (page 232)*

Unless you have a pressure cooker, soak beans in boiling water and stand overnight. Pour this water off and cook the daffas for about 2 hours; broad and runner beans will take much less time so watch them after 45 minutes. Use plenty of water but no salt. Drain well and put through a sieve. They should be of a dry consistency. Chop onions and cut up leeks finely. Grate carrot. Crush garlic.

Cook onions, carrot, leek and garlic in oil until soft. Add salt, pepper and herbs. Add chopped or well drained bottled tomatoes, beans and oats or wheat. Mix well. Beat egg and add. Liberally butter a fireproof dish. Pour in mixture. Bake for 1 hour at 350°F. Top with the grated cheese after 45 minutes.

This makes a pleasant roast dinner, so serve with roast potatoes, roast parsnips, carrots and a green vegetable and vegetarian 'gravy' (page 146).

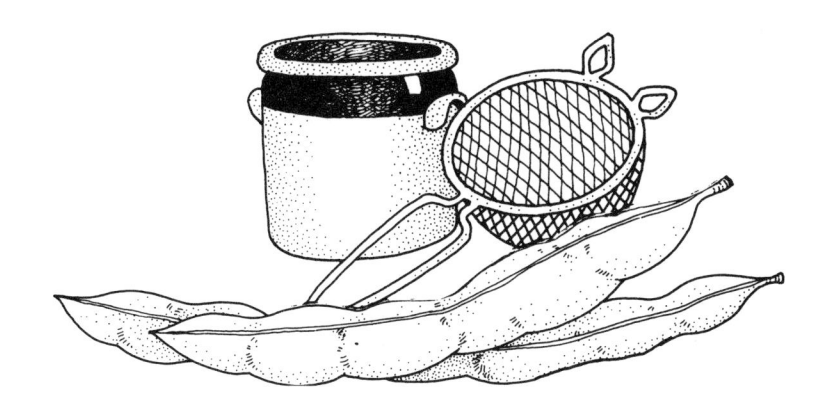

Stuffed Green Peppers

The distinctive flavour of Stilton cheese makes this recipe a little special. Not that green peppers are in the luxury bracket, for they will grow in Britain out of doors in most gardens, and thrive in unheated greenhouses.

4 peppers
1 lb tomatoes
½ lb fresh wholemeal breadcrumbs
¼ lb Stilton cheese
1 egg
1 oz. butter or oil
Little stock
2 teaspoonsful fresh or dried basil
Salt and freshly ground black pepper

Wash and wipe peppers, then cut off tops with a sharp knife. Set aside. Carefully remove seeds and white membrane. Heat butter or oil in pan and cook tomatoes for a few minutes to reduce water content. Cut up Stilton and work into breadcrumbs. Add tomato, basil, beaten egg, salt and pepper to taste, and mix thoroughly. Divide mixture among the prepared peppers. Pop the tops back on and place in a oven-to-table dish with about ½ inch of good vegetable stock in bottom. If dish is not deep enough for a lid, cover with foil. Cook in pre-heated 350°F oven for 30 minutes. When cooked the peppers should be firm.

Stuffed Baked Potatoes

An appetising meatless lunch dish, based on the balanced nourishment of our old, friendly winter standby.

4 medium sized potatoes
2 tablespoonsful of your favourite chutney
¼ lb cottage cheese or grated Cheddar
Little butter or oil
Pepper and salt

Scrub potatoes and dry. Put a small amount of oil or butter in palm of hand and work into each potato. Bake in moderate oven until soft when a skewer inserted – an hour or more. Cut into two halves lengthways, scoop out the flesh with a sharp spoon and put into a mixing bowl. Have ready an ovenproof dish that will take all the skin cases laid side by side. Mix well potato, cheese, chutney and salt and pepper to taste. Pile into waiting cases, dot with butter and return in dish to oven until nicely browned. Serve with a salad such as raw beetroot or coleslaw.

Optional variations:
Herbs, chives, grated onion and beaten egg are just a few examples of alternative fillings.

Britain's dogs and cats eat a million tons of meat and meat products a year. Much of this 'mountain' is clean and wholesome – enough to feed each one of us a pound of meat a week.

Potato Cheese Casserole with Cider

In winter through to early spring you'll enjoy the piquancy which cheese and cider bring to the humble potato in this warming meatless dish. Potatoes need not be perfect.

4 medium potatoes
2 large onions
½ lb grated cheese
½ pint dry cider
Little butter
Pepper and salt

Scrub potatoes, cut into thin slices, wash in colander under running tap and drain. Grate cheese and save 3 tablespoonsful for top. Prepare onion, cutting into very thin slices. Butter a large casserole dish, then place ingredients in, layer by layer beginning with potatoes, then onion, then cheese and some seasoning. Repeat layers until dish is full, finishing with a potato layer. Pour over the cider, sprinkle with remaining cheese and cook in a slow oven for 1½ to 2 hours until mushed.
Enhanced if served with hot wholemeal herb bread and a large salad – raw grated beetroot or carrot, or green.

Surprise Potatoes

Appearances do count! You can eat this dish, either with eggs or as a meat extender, winter or summer, and its attractive looks disguise its simplicity and economy.

1 medium potato for each person
1 egg for each person
Little butter, margarine or oil
Fresh parsley
Salt and pepper

Scrub potatoes. Dry and coat with a little fat or oil. Bake as for jacket potatoes. When cooked, take a sharp knife and cut out a good sized hole from side of each potato. Lightly salt and pepper each hole and pop in a small amount of butter and a sprinkling of chopped parsley. Break into hole a small egg. Sprinkle on top a little more parsley and add a touch more butter. Mash scooped out potato with little butter, salt and pepper, then pile round opening, allowing egg to show. Return to oven for 7 to 12 minutes – until egg is set.

Optional variation:
In place of egg use minced cooked cold meats. Put meat into a thick gravy or white sauce (page 190). Spoon into potato cases while piping hot. Return to oven for 10 minutes to brown the edges.

Spinach Bake

You can serve this meatless dish in late autumn and again in early spring, for spinach and swiss chard survive all but the more vicious frosts – and possibly even those if protected by cloches. But it won't merely help you at those times; you can enjoy it any time in summer, when these prolific vegetables quickly recover from each picking.

A large bunch spinach or swiss chard
3 eggs
½ lb cottage cheese
3 tablespoonsful milk
1 medium onion
Little oil or butter
2 teaspoonsful fresh or dried rosemary or a little nutmeg if preferred
1 small clove garlic
Salt and pepper

Wash spinach or chard carefully in several waters. If using spinach pull off and discard its tough stalks; if swiss chard cut off juicy thick white stems to eat as a separate vegetable. In either case, break up leaves and cook until tender, slowly at first. Just the water left on leaves after washing should be adequate, for they release juices as they cook. When cooked drain off any excess juice to save for soup stock – or drink it right away! The greens should now be fairly dry. Chop onion into small pieces and cook in oil or butter until soft but not browned. Mix in crushed garlic. Beat eggs until fluffy. Add sieved cheese, milk, rosemary or nutmeg, and salt and pepper to taste. Mix in cooked spinach or chard. Butter a 7 inch soufflé dish and pour in mixture. Pour 1 inch of boiling water into a baking dish and cook your spinach bake like a custard in pre-heated moderate oven for about 45 minutes – until set and golden. Serve with jacket potatoes, grilled tomatoes – if available – and perhaps a raw carrot salad (page 98).

Stuffed Tomatoes

Enjoy this meatless dish hot or cold. Useful when tomatoes are plentiful and cheap.

4 large firm, ripe tomatoes
2 eggs
1 flat tablespoonful 81% flour
2 tablespoonsful milk
1 heaped tablespoonful chopped fresh parsley and rosemary mixed, or basil, savory and chives. Or a mixture of your favourite fresh herbs
Salt and pepper
Little oil

Cut a slice from the top of the tomato. Take out seeds and pulp carefully so as not to break cases. Oil an oven-to-table dish and put in tomato cases. Beat eggs with milk then mix flour with chopped inside of tomatoes, add with herbs and seasoning to eggs. Pour into tomato cases. Bake in fairly hot oven 400°F until egg is set – about 15 to 20 minutes.

Stalks of swiss chard are delicious cooked in a very little water until just tender. When cooked they should be crisp. Takes about 6 minutes. Toss in butter with lots of black pepper or a dash of nutmeg. Or cover with white sauce.

Vegetable Casserole

The casserole is your opportunity to create dishes of splendid variety, for as you become bolder you can experiment with pieces of this and a dash or two of that. Wonderful for absorbing gluts, the casserole is satisfying on its own, while being invaluable for making meat go further. This dumpling-enriched recipe will help to see you through a long winter – but treat it as a foundation on which to build.

2 medium onions
2 leeks
1 medium swede
2 medium carrots
1 medium parsnip
1 small celeriac
½ pint stock or water
Gravy mix
2 tablespoonsful oil
Bay leaf
4 cloves
1 teaspoonful mixed dried herbs
1 teaspoonful yeast extract
Salt and pepper to taste
Dumplings (page 243)

Scrub carrots, parsnip, swede and celeriac or celery, cutting out any bad parts. Cut into ½ inch chunks. (Celery seeds can replace celeriac or celery). Peel and slice onion. Wash leeks extra well and cut into pieces. Heat oil in 3 pint flame-proof casserole, iron or enamelled. Put root vegetables in and work with wooden fork until golden and the natural juices start to come – about 5-10 minutes, stirring all the time. Add leeks and onions, bay leaf, cloves and pepper. Mix in well over low heat without burning the vegetables. Cook with lid on for 5 more minutes. Make up the gravy

MAINLY MAIN DISHES

with water or stock or juice from tomatoes and 2 to 3 teaspoonsful gravy mix. Combine with vegetables. Lastly work in yeast extract evenly without breaking up vegetables, which should stay crisp when cooked. Place in bottom of oven with lid on to keep warm.

Make the dumplings and divide the mixture into 4. Take casserole out of oven. Bring vegetables to boil, arrange dumplings evenly on top of them. Cook either on top of stove on gentle heat or in pre-heated oven for 15 minutes or until dumplings are fluffy. Serve immediately.

Optional variations:
½ pint juice from bottled tomatoes
3 sticks celery
1 teaspoonful celery seed

Bean Rissoles

This meatless dish tastes so 'meaty' that some would never know! The old English field bean, which has made a modest comeback as the 'daffa' or 'tic', has a characteristic flavour that few people know today. Most welcome during winter and early spring.

*2 cupsful cooked sieved daffa beans
(about 12 oz. dried)
1 medium onion
2 tablespoonsful cooked barley
1 tablespoonful porridge oats
1 teaspoonful salt, freshly ground black pepper
½ teaspoonful tabasco
Clove garlic
1 teaspoonful mixed herbs
Little oil*

Drain the beans, then sieve them while still hot into a big enough bowl to mix. They should be as dry as possible. Chop the onion fine. Add to the beans with the barley, seasoning, oats, mixed herbs and garlic and combine thoroughly. Take a strong fry pan and pour in a little oil to coat the surface. Heat the pan over moderate heat. Drop spoonfuls of the mixture into the pan and press down, cooking each side for about 5 to 6 minutes until nicely browned. Keep hot until all the mixture is used up. Serve with a rich brown gravy.

Bean Spread

You can eat this tasty concoction like paté, on wholemeal toast or oatmeal biscuits; or with a green salad in place of cheese. Its base is daffa, tic or field beans – nutty, almost 'meaty' – which you can grow yourself and enjoy any month of the year.

1 lb cooked daffa, tic or field beans
Large clove garlic
4 shakes of tabasco – more if preferred
Salt and pepper
Little melted butter

Drain beans well and while still warm pass through a sieve into a large bowl to remove skins. Should weigh 1 lb when sieved. Crush garlic into beans and add pepper, salt and tabasco, check for seasoning to taste, then beat all well together. Place in a dish, smooth over the top and pour on a little melted butter to cover. Keep in a cold place, no longer than 3 days.

Most of the people in the Poor South lack clean water and sanitation. To provide these essentials would mean an investment of about four billion pounds a year for ten years. This sounds a lot, but it is less than a tenth of what the Rich North spends on alcohol.

Vegetarian 'Gravy'

Here's how we make a flavoursome vegetarian 'gravy' from vegetables, herbs and a basic proprietary gravy mix.

½ *pint juice from bottled tomatoes*
or vegetable stock (page 236)
1 small onion
½ teaspoonful mixed herbs ·
3 teaspoonsful gravy mix
½ teaspoonful yeast extract if liked
Salt and pepper

Prepare and chop onion very fine, then cook in the juice or stock until tender. Blend gravy mix with a little stock and, if using yeast extract, mix in thoroughly ½ teaspoonful with rest of ingredients and cook for a few minutes until thickened. Add more stock if necessary, adjust seasoning and then strain.

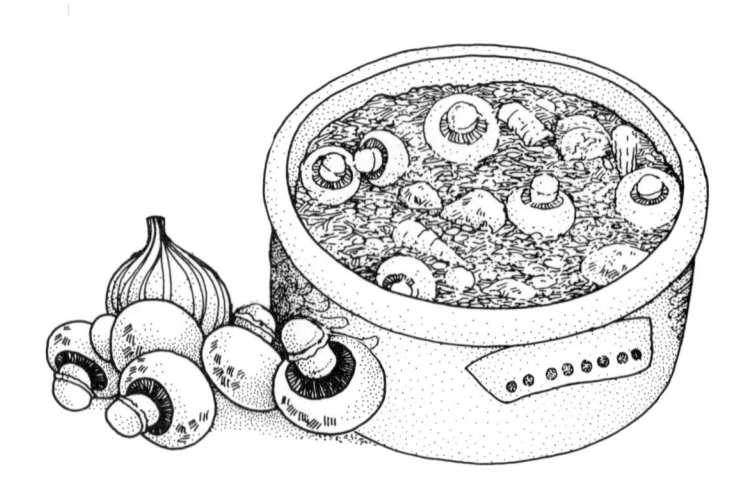

Baked Barley

A nourishing, filling dish especially appreciated on chilly days. Tempting without meat, or even more so when combined with any left-over meat. You'll need a large casserole dish with lid.

1 small cup pearl barley
2 oz. butter or oil
6 oz. fresh mushrooms
2 medium onions
2 tablespoonsful shredded green tops of leek
1 cup bottled or fresh tomatoes, skinned
4 cups good stock to your liking
(same cups as for barley)

Wash and cut up mushrooms and cook in 1 cup of stock for about 5 minutes. Cut up onions finely into half moons and sauté in fry pan in half the butter until golden and limp. Transfer with a slotted spoon onto mushrooms. Add remaining butter to fry pan and sauté barley over low heat until a rich golden colour – about 8 minutes. Onto barley pour 1 cup of hot stock and the tomatoes. Transfer this, with onions, mushrooms and leek, to well-buttered casserole. Add another cup of stock and cook for 30 minutes with lid on in 350°F oven, or on top of stove, simmering very gently and ensuring the barley is not sticking. After 30 minutes add the 2 other cups of hot stock, stirring in gently so as not to mush the vegetables. Then cook uncovered for another 15 minutes. Serve with a green salad to complement it.

Optional variation:
At the same time as the final stock add 2 cups of minced left-over meat, cooking until heated through.

Cheese and Eggs Galore

Here are some recipes based on eggs or cheese, or both. Some include vegetables and some don't, but either way we hope they stimulate your imagination for more ideas.

Savoury Poached Eggs

Eggs with carefully married flavours – fresh from the garden if you're lucky. Will make either a light meal or a main one.

4 eggs
1 lb ripe tomatoes
1 large onion
2 green peppers
2 teaspoonsful basil
1 clove garlic
1 tablespoonful oil
Salt and pepper

Prepare onion and cut into very thin slices. Heat oil in a fry pan or, if you have one, a flameproof, shallow oven-to-table dish, and cook onion for a few minutes. Pop tomatoes into boiling water for a couple of minutes, then into cold to remove skins. Slice and add to onions. From peppers remove seeds and white membrane and cut into thin strips. Add to pan or dish last with crushed garlic clove, basil and freshly ground black pepper. Cook for a few minutes only – onion and pepper should remain crisp. Break each egg separately into a cup and place carefully in 4 separate places over the mixture. Simmer gently with a lid on until eggs are poached. Serve at once with toast, or make into a main meal with creamed potatoes and a green side salad.

Stuffed Eggs in Wine Sauce

Herbs and spices combine with wine to create an egg dish on those wintry days that call for something slightly special.

4 or 6 hard boiled eggs
¾ pint white sauce (page 190)
Some mayonnaise (page 105 or 106)
Little butter
1 small garlic clove
Little white wine
1 teaspoonful fresh rosemary
or mixed herbs
Chopped parsley
Salt and pepper

Cut eggs lengthways and remove yolks. Mash them in a bowl with crushed garlic, finely chopped rosemary or mixed herbs, salt and pepper to taste, and enough mayonnaise to moisten the yolks. Fill the whites with the mixture and lay in a shallow, buttered oven-to-table dish or in individual dishes, two halves to each person. Make the sauce fairly thick and beat in 2 tablespoonful white wine, then pour over eggs. Put in moderate oven for 10 minutes or under a slow grill until the sauce is golden and bubbling. Decorate with chopped parsley.

Diseases of obesity are not the only cost of over-eating. Drugs to suppress appetite cost the National Health Service – that is, the taxpayer – £3 million a year.

Savoury Batter

Plenty of delicate flavours in this popular meatless dish.

For the batter:–
6 oz. wholemeal flour
(or ½ white, ½ wholemeal)
½ pint fresh or sour milk
(or ½ milk, ½ water)
1 egg
2 oz. grated cheese
1 teaspoonful baking powder
2 tablespoonsful oil
Small clove garlic
Fresh rosemary

For the filling:–
½ lb very small tomatoes
6 small onions
1 large leek (white part only)
¼ lb button mushrooms

If you have a blender make batter in it by putting egg, milk, garlic, rosemary, salt and baking powder in first, flour last. Blend for ½ minute, then with spatula push down any unmixed flour, add 1 tablespoonful of the oil and blend another ½ minute. Leave to stand for at least 1 hour. Have a fairly hot oven going. Put the other tablespoonful oil in a 10-inch shallow dish to pre-heat. Skin tomatoes and leave whole. Cut onions into halves or quarters depending on size. Wash and cut leek into 1 inch pieces. Wash mushrooms, then toss them with leek and onion in a pan with very little oil for about 5 minutes to part cook – keep them moving. Pour batter into the hot dish and place the vegetables and mushrooms in a design over the top. Cook for 30 minutes on middle shelf. Then sprinkle over grated cheese and return to oven for 10 minutes until cheese is melted and golden. Serve at once – preferably with a green salad and grated carrot salad, or creamed spinach and braised carrots.

Savoury Pancake Layers

This 'one dish' meal in which herbs complement pancakes, satisfies any craving for 'richness' without being at all lavish with rich ingredients.

For the Pancakes:–
6 oz. sieved wholemeal or 81% flour
2 eggs
¾ pint milk
2 tablespoonsful oil
½ teaspoonful salt
1 teaspoonful baking powder

Combine flour, salt, baking powder in large bowl. Separate eggs – whites into large dry bowl – beat yolks into milk. Make a smooth batter in the usual way, adding oil with milk and egg mixture, then set aside for at least 1 hour. Or use a blender for quickness. Just before you make pancakes fold in stiffly beaten whites.

For the Filling:–
1 lb prepared and cooked spinach
½ lb cottage cheese
½ lb skinned and chopped tomatoes
2 teaspoonsful mixed fresh herbs,
such as rosemary, thyme, marjoram,
basil and some mint
1 clove garlic
1 tablespoonful oil
1 large onion
2 oz. grated tasty cheese
Some paprika
Salt and freshly ground black pepper
About 1 pint white sauce (p 190)
with small crushed clove garlic

Prepare spinach and cook as dry as possible. Remove any excess moisture and chop. Keep hot. Slice onion very thin and with the tomato cook in oil until soft. Crush garlic and add to tomato and onion mixture, then add mixed herbs but not mint. Season with salt and pepper. Combine thoroughly cottage cheese, mint and spinach, and season to taste. Now give batter a final beat and make into six or eight pancakes in usual way. Keep hot.

Butter a deep, round oven-to-table dish. Cover the base with some of tomato mixture, then a pancake, then a layer of spinach mixture, then another pancake. Spoon over some of tomato mixture and continue in this way using up all spinach mixture between pancakes. Finish with a pancake. If any tomato mixture is left, pour down the sides. Pour over the sauce, scatter grated cheese evenly over top, and dust with paprika. Put in preheated 350°F oven until bubbling and the top nicely browned – about 30-45 minutes.

Serve by cutting in wedges like a cake to show the separate layers.

Cheese Flan

If you're among the fortunate few with enough land to keep a goat or two, or a house cow, you'll need some ideas on using the abundance of excellent curd or cottage cheese which you can make – and hard cheese too if you're a house cow family. Best of all we rate cheese flan, not least because it is capable of so many variations. Mind you, there's no need to take up dairying just to make it! Bought cheese will do almost as well. Here is our recipe for a basic cheese and onion flan, followed by some suggestions for ringing the changes.

½ lb curd or cottage cheese
3 tablespoonsful single cream or milk
3 eggs
1 fresh or pickled shallot
Small clove of garlic
1 teaspoonful dry mustard
½ teaspoonful or more of salt
Pepper
1 teaspoonful fresh rosemary
2 medium onions
1 tablespoonful oil or butter

Optional variations:
¼ lb tasty cheese, grated
Tomatoes
2 fat leeks
Sweet corn
Green pepper
Mushrooms
Bacon
Left-over cooked ham, tongue, chicken or fish

Line a 9-inch flan form with plain shortcrust pastry (See page 210). Prick base and partially bake in moderate oven. Cook finely sliced onion in oil or butter until soft and golden. Spread over pastry case. Put the rest of the basic ingredients in blender and run for 1 minute. (If you have no blender, put the curd or cottage cheese into a large bowl with a little of the beaten egg and cream or milk, mash and beat until smooth. Blend the mustard also with a little of the egg, add other ingredients, rest of egg and finely chopped rosemary). Pour mixture over the onion in flan case, decorate with tomato rings, and bake in centre of moderate 350°F oven until set and golden in colour. Let flan stand 10 minutes before serving. It is just as good cold.

As we've suggested, you'll find fascinating scope for variations on the theme of cheese flan, and we've listed a few tested extra ingredients as a starting point. Obviously they don't all go in one flan! However you can confidently put in more than one at a time if you wish. One point: you will find that you'll get best results by making adjustments to the basic recipe, for example by omitting the onions if you use leeks. Also if you fancy grated tasty cheese, better halve the amount of curd or cottage. Incidentally your result will be even tastier if you fold half the grated cheese into the mixture (or add it to the blender) and sprinkle the other half on top to form a crust. Remember too that this flan is a first class way of making meat or fish go further.

Meat and Fish

Recipes using meat and fish come next. One group of meat recipes is based on British wild animals. These of course can be the cleanest of natural foods, and to anyone with understandable qualms, we would add that these animals do have to be culled, and if culled then eaten. They represent an important source of protein.

There are estimated to be 5,000,000 pigeons in Britain. If we were to crop half that amount each year, we would add about a million pounds weight of meat to our diet. You'll find a recipe for casserole of pigeon on page 164.

In the Highlands of Scotland alone there are 200,000 red deer. To prevent over-grazing and keep the herds well-fed, about 30,000 are killed each year. No meat could be healthier. It is delicious when hung for a while before eating, and for those who have access to it we have given a recipe on page 168 for a venison casserole.

Wild rabbit may be hard to come by, although since its near-extermination by myxomatosis in 1953 the species is making a gradual come-back. You wouldn't eat an afflicted wild rabbit, for any signs of the disease are obvious, especially in the liver. Rabbit is good, wholesome food and many people breed their own for the table. We've given just two of the many ways to cook rabbit on pages 165 and 166.

Large quantities of trout are produced in fish farms, but they are usually fed high protein pellets, the basis of which comes from the Poor South, which is why we haven't given any recipes. However, since they are a carnivorous fish they could be fed on blood and offal waste from the slaughter houses. They are unlikely to be a cheap source of protein, but you can still enjoy them on special occasions. They are delicious grilled, served with parsley butter.

Beef and Ham Roll

Yet another way of making meat go farther, this old family favourite of ours is great for summer salads and children's school lunches. It's easy to make and considerably less expensive than the bought variety, with guarantee of no preservatives or other additives! Note that it makes use of breadcrumbs – a handy ingredient for a host of recipes designed for meat economy. If you haven't a mincer, make sure that the mince you buy is your butcher's very best quality.

1 lb lean beef
½ lb lean ham or bacon
½ lb breadcrumbs
1 egg
½ teaspoonful thyme
1 teaspoonful parsley
½ teaspoonful pepper
1 teaspoonful salt

Finely mince ham (or bacon) and beef. In a bowl, combine meat, herbs, seasoning and breadcrumbs. Beat egg and work well into ingredients. If it seems dry, add a little water, though remember that the meat will make its own juices. Well butter a pudding basin. Alternatively if you have an old fashioned stone 2 lb marmalade jar, use that. Press mixture well down with spoon. Cover securely with plenty of butter paper. Cook for 2 hours in gently boiling water like pudding. Leave in container until cold, then ease out with a sharp knife. Keep in fridge or very cool place.

Boiled Fowl with Bacon and Herbs

About the most basic of several ways to make a good meal out of a laying hen past her prime. It really will taste of chicken – more so that any young bird. It's economical too, and even more so if cooked in a pressure cooker – about 45 minutes, but check with your handbook first.

1 fowl
Piece of boiling bacon
or 4 pieces of streaky bacon
1 large carrot
1 medium onion
1 small turnip or swede
Some outside celery sticks
Large bunch mixed fresh herbs
or 2 teaspoonsful dried herbs
1 bay leaf
6 peppercorns
Boiling water
1 pint rich parsley sauce (page 190)

If using a piece of bacon soak overnight. Afterwards clean well and add to pan with fowl. Stand trussed fowl on a rack or upturned saucer in bottom of pan so as to keep bird clear of bottom. Pour on enough boiling water to cover up to top of legs. Add prepared vegetables, soaked bacon and herbs. Put lid on and simmer very gently for an hour, then take off heat. Very carefully turn fowl onto its side so that breast is covered and continue cooking gently until tender. This will take a further hour or less depending on age of bird. Take off heat and let stand in water for 15 minutes. Remove fowl, making sure no stock water remains inside, place on a serving dish and keep warm.

Remove bacon, cut into slices and place round bird. If using streaky bacon, cut pieces into 2 or 3, roll them, then grill or fry till crisp and golden and place round bird. Make the rich parsley sauce. Coat bird with some of it before taking to table and serve rest separately. Garnish with parsley and watercress. Save vegetables and water – now stock – for soup another day, or for a basic aspic jelly (overleaf).

To save time make more of a sauce than you need for just one recipe. You can keep it in the fridge for making up a quick dish later.

Galantine of Chicken

You don't have to eat boiling fowl hot, as this galantine recipe shows.

1 cooked boiling fowl
Stock from the cooked fowl
½ oz. gelatine
2 tablespoonsful cider vinegar
Salt and pepper

Remove all breast meat and tender meat from wing section, thighs and the 'oysters'. (The recipe after this suggests one way of using the rest of the meat.) Cut this best meat into elongated serving pieces and set aside.

Strain through a fine sieve the broth in which you cooked the bird. Pour into a heavy pan and boil fast to reduce its volume to ¾ pint. Pour into a bowl and let it stand for 30 minutes. By then the fat will have risen and you can gently pour it off or skim with a tablespoon.

Make a very basic aspic jelly by dissolving in a pan ½ oz. of gelatine in a little of the stock, pour on the rest of the stock adding 2 tablespoonsful cider vinegar.

Adjust seasoning to taste. Strain into a clean bowl through a piece of fine muslin. Wet an oval Pyrex dish as for a jelly. Pour in a small amount of aspic to cover bottom, place some of the best looking pieces of meat into this and pour over a little more aspic – just enough to cover meat. Let stand in a cool place till almost set, then add rest of meat and aspic, which should now be cold but not set. Leave until all is set stiff. Turn out onto a flat serving dish, big enough for you to decorate with lettuce, watercress and tomato.

Serve with a dressing on the side, potato salad (page 102) and any other raw salad you fancy. If you want to make this dish really festive you can make a pattern of cooked peas, tomato rounds without seeds or cucumber in the first layer of the mould before adding meat and aspic.

Optional Variation:
If you like the idea of a cream galantine, reduce the stock to ½ pint and proceed as above. After you have strained the aspic through a fine muslin leave to cool and add ¼ pint of thin cream. Pour over the prepared chicken in the Pyrex dish. When set turn out as before and decorate.

Chicken Mayonnaise

Strip the rest of the meat from the carcase and coarsely mince. Add some mayonnaise, chopped parsley and chives and serve garnished on open slices of wholemeal bread or as a sandwich filling for children's school lunches. Put the carcase in a pan, breaking it up first, just cover with water and simmer for an hour or use the pressure cooker to get some more stock.

The home freezer is one of the great wasters of time, money and energy this century, ruining the texture of vegetables and impairing flavour. In all but extreme northern latitudes it is usually unnecessary, for elsewhere you can enjoy adequate, British-grown fresh vegetables all-year round, grown without cloche or greenhouse. Once you become accustomed to 'imitation' fresh vegetables and fruit at any time, you can no longer look forward to, or enjoy, the real thing with equal zest. Enthusiasts point to the seasonal surpluses it saves. Sound planning however can largely prevent surpluses, and, when they do occur, donations, drying and bottling, can usually solve any problems. The waste of resources in making and running the freezer is seldom justified by saving the occasional leftovers.

Cornish Pasties

This meat-extending recipe was given to us by a friend who has used it for years. We've suggested making it with breast of lamb or mutton because it's a relatively cheap cut which butchers seem to find hard to sell. Anyway, it suits this old fashioned recipe admirably. First cut away all excess fat from the breast and use it to make dripping. Cut up the lean meat very finely or mince it.

Minced meat from breast of lamb or mutton
1 medium potato, grated
1 medium onion cut up very fine, or a fat leek sliced into thin circles and chopped
1 small swede, grated
Plenty of chopped parsley
Salt and pepper
Little gravy or water to moisten

Combine all the ingredients listed above thoroughly. Make ½ lb wholemeal pastry (page 210). Stand for 30 minutes and keep it cool while making filling. Divide pastry into 6 or 8 portions and roll out on well floured surface to rounds about the size of saucers. Divide the filling among them, placing it over one half. Dampen edges, fold over and press down well with thumb to seal. Make a small incision in the top of each to let out steam. Place on a baking sheet in 400°F oven for 10 minutes, then reduce to 325°F or move lower down oven and bake for 45 to 50 minutes.

Roast Stuffed Shoulder of Mutton or Lamb

One of the less exciting cuts of meat gains flavour and serves more when cooked this way. Delicious cold too. Have your butcher bone the shoulder or, if you are able, do it yourself.

Fill the pocket left with either ½ quantity of chestnut stuffing (page 189) or forcemeat (page 188). Tie with string or fasten with small stainless steel skewers. Rub a little salt and freshly ground pepper onto outside of meat. Place filled side down on a little fat in baking dish. Cover with some butter paper. Cook in brisk oven for 30 minutes to seal the meat. Reduce heat to 300°F and cook slowly, covered for a further 1 hour 30 minutes or more, depending on size of joint. Add some red wine to the pan when you make the gravy.

Tin or aluminium foil is made from a finite resource and demands too much energy in its manufacture to be used once and thrown away. So try to use sparingly and repeatedly – if use it you must. If you have a dish without a lid and you can't replace it, tin foil is a useful substitute.

To prevent a joint of meat losing weight and shrinking while cooking always use a covered baking dish. It also keeps the oven clean. Always let the cooked joint stand for 15 minutes before carving to 'set'. It can then be cut in thinner slices and will go further.

Casserole of Pigeons with Red Wine

Many a gardener and farmer would swear that the proper place for a pigeon is in the pot. In this recipe the traditional imported wine is replaced by homemade elderberry or plum.

*2 pigeons, young if possible
(older ones take much longer to cook)
2 slices streaky bacon
½ pint elderberry or rich plum wine
1 oz. butter
1 medium onion
12 small onions
1 tablespoonful flour
¼ lb mushrooms
Bay leaf
1 teaspoonful fresh or dried thyme
2 tablespoonsful finely chopped parsley
Salt and freshly ground black pepper*

Cut the dressed pigeons into two.
Mix flour and seasonings together and coat pigeon pieces. Cut bacon into inch pieces and cook in heavy fry pan or flame-proof casserole until golden. Remove and set aside. Add butter and brown the pigeon pieces. Remove and set aside. Cook chopped onion in the juices, add remaining flour mixture, and work to a smooth paste. Add wine, bay leaf and thyme. Replace pigeon, breast side down, and bacon. Cover and cook in slow oven at 300 to 325°F for about 2 hours. If you prepared this in a fry pan then of course transfer to a heated oven-to-table dish. Cook the small onions and mushrooms, sliced if necessary, in a little red wine for about 10 minutes. Before serving, turn pigeon pieces breast side up, add onions and mushrooms to the casserole and heat for a few minutes. When ready to serve adjust the seasoning to taste and sprinkle with chopped parsley. Serve from the casserole.

Roast Rabbit

Here is a dish for special occasions, made succulent by the use of cream – though not so rich as it may seem when you consider that it works out at just three tablespoonsful for each celebrant.

1 young rabbit
8 small onions
Forcemeat (page 188)
½ pint cream

Prepare the rabbit and wash and dry well, making sure there are no hairs left on the flesh. Cut off head if you prefer. Put forcemeat into stomach cavity, wrap over the flaps and skewer to keep in place. (Use either wooden toothpicks or small sized stainless steel skewers.) Lay rabbit stomach-down in a sitting position in baking dish. Pour over cream and arrange onions around.
Cook for about 1 hour covered in a moderate oven, basting with cream regularly so that meat doesn't become dry. Test with knife. Remove onto a hot serving dish and arrange onions around. Pour over cream juices from the baking dish. Stick a small bunch of parsley in the front of the rabbit.
Serve with jacket potatoes, sprouts or other green vegetables and carrots, as well as elderberry and crabapple jelly or redcurrant jelly.

Save the wrapping paper butter comes in, but not the foil type. Keep in the fridge to use for lining cake tins, or putting on top of the breast of a chicken when roasting. Saves tin foil.

Casserole of Rabbit

If you rear your own rabbits, or you can obtain fresh young ones, try this casserole, which is both tasty and economical.

1 young rabbit
½ pint rabbit or chicken stock
2 oz. flour
2 oz. butter or 1 tablespoonful corn oil
Little milk
Large onion
2 teaspoonsful fresh thyme
1 teaspoonful fresh lemon balm or
2 teaspoonsful dried mixed herbs
2 tablespoonsful parsley
Pepper and salt
4 pieces of streaky bacon

Clean and wash the rabbit and dry well, making sure it finishes free from hairs. Joint it carefully for the bones are rather brittle. You will have two shoulder joints, two back leg joints and a good piece of back and neck. The rest of the ribs and flappy bits can go into the stockpot. (If you rear your own, there will be other parts, such as the head, which can also go into the stockpot).
Cover the discarded pieces with water and simmer for an hour, or pressure-cook for about 20 minutes. Have oven ready at 300°F and heat a 2-pint casserole dish. Put the flour, herbs, pepper, salt on a plate and mix well. Dip the prepared joints of rabbit in the milk, and shake off excess and coat in the flour mixture.
Heat butter or oil in a fry pan and brown pieces on both sides. Put rabbit pieces into heated casserole dish. Add thinly sliced onion to fry pan and brown gently – do not burn. Sprinkle over the rabbit.
Cut rind from bacon, cut into two and roll up. Place between rabbit pieces.

Put the left-over flour and herb mixture into the fry pan
and make gravy with the stock. Adjust seasoning to
taste. Pour over the rabbit and cook covered for 45
minutes to 1 hour or until rabbit is soft to the touch
of a knife. Just before serving, garnish with
the chopped parsley.
Serve with jacket potatoes, cooked at the same time,
with a green vegetable and carrots for colour.

Venison Casserole

A dish for 'feast days' with an ecological *rationale*! The deer thrives on land fit only for wild creatures, providing protein from natural herbs, uncontaminated by feed additives or injections.

1½ lb venison steak
½ lb best quality stewing steak
4 slices streaky bacon
½ pint red wine
¼ pint or less of stock (page 236)
1 bay leaf
8 small onions
4 cloves
Flour
Salt and pepper
Bacon fat, butter or oil
Forcemeat (page 188)
1 teaspoonful mixed herbs

Cut meat into inch cubes, toss in flour and brown in melted fat in fry pan. Transfer to casserole dish. Cut rind from streaky bacon, cut each piece in 2 or 4, depending on length, and roll up. Place rolls between meat in dish. Peel onions and place a clove into 4 of them. Then arrange *all* onions evenly round the dish. Make a thick gravy with rest of flour, fry pan juices and red wine. Add stock if necessary, freshly ground pepper and salt to taste and pour over the meat. Sprinkle with herbs. Cover and cook in a moderate oven for 2 to 2½ hours. Roll forcemeat into balls and push into gravy about 20 minutes before serving time.
Serve with jacket potatoes, carrots and a green vegetable and redcurrant jelly.

Meat Balls

Not only will these make meat go farther, they will make other dishes even more appetising.

¾ lb minced lean beef
¼ lb minced pork
¼ lb fresh breadcrumbs
1 egg
2 tablespoonsful oil
2 tablespoonsful chopped parsley
Large clove garlic if liked
Some flour
Salt and freshly ground pepper

Combine very well the meat breadcrumbs, parsley, salt, pepper, garlic and lightly beaten egg. Stand for 30 minutes. Form into small balls and toss in flour. A good idea is to put some flour into a bag and toss the balls in it, a few at a time. Heat oil in a strong frypan and brown the balls on all sides – about 10 to 15 minutes.
Remove from the pan and keep hot.
You can add meat balls to any one of a number of recipes, for instance: to the pasta sauce on page 191, or the vegetable casserole on page 142.

In a survey on attitudes to food and health, nearly half the women interviewed said their husbands would complain if they served a meal without meat or fish. Eating meat is psychologically an expression of power and manliness, essentially a masculine food! The Small Island Diet is a step to liberation from sexism.

Shepherd's Pie

In this recipe we include vegetables to help the meat go farther and make the crust with the celeriac croquette mixture on page 126. The ingredients enhance each other's flavour handsomely.

Some minced cooked mutton or lamb
1 medium swede
1 medium onion
1 medium carrot
Some gravy
Celeriac and potato topping
Some mixed herbs
Little butter or oil

Scrub and grate coarsely swede and carrot. Chop onion. Melt butter or oil in pan and cook vegetables, stirring continuously until soft and golden – about 5 minutes. Using left-over gravy and stock, mix the vegetables, minced mutton and mixed herbs together. Transfer to a pie dish and top with the celeriac croquette mixture, which need not be cooled for this recipe. Cook in hot oven until top is crisp and brown – about 20 minutes.

Optional variations:
Although traditionally shepherd's pie is made – not surprisingly – with mutton, no one will mind if you make your pie with minced beef. Except perhaps the occasional shepherd...

Fresh minced meat can of course be used. If so, cook it first for 10 minutes, stirring occasionally, to release the fat. Take the meat from the pan with a slotted spoon and set aside. If there is an excess of fat, pour off and leave only enough to cook the vegetables. Make some gravy with stock and then carry on as for the cooked meat recipe.

Tripe in Cider

Much maligned, constantly ridiculed, this easily digested source of iron and other nutrients can be an economical delicacy. Try breaking the tripe barrier with this recipe.

1 lb dressed tripe
1 large onion
4 medium carrots
½ pint cider
1 clove of garlic
1 bay leaf
1 teaspoonful mixed herbs
Little butter
Little flour
Salt and pepper

Wash tripe well then put into cold water and bring to the boil. Remove and when cool enough cut into small thin strips. Slice onion into half moons. Scrub carrots and cut into thin rounds. Put a knob of butter into a medium sized pan and toss tripe in it for a few minutes. Add vegetables, herbs, crushed garlic and seasoning. Pour over cider and simmer gently for 2 hours. If you already have the oven going you can cook it in a casserole dish instead. Thicken just before serving if necessary. Serve with creamed potatoes to which you have added 2 tablespoonsful finely chopped parsley.

Baked Smoked Mackerel

The piquancy of this recipe will be especially appreciated in winter or early spring when cooking repertoires benefit from a little imagination.

4 pieces of smoked mackerel
White sauce (page 190)
Chopped parsley
Some capers
Some fresh horseradish
1 teaspoonful made mustard

Place mackerel onto a shallow enamelled plate and bake in slow oven to release excess oil. When oil released and tops are crisp, transfer carefully to a hot serving dish. Meanwhile make ½ pint of white sauce to which you have added the mustard and 1 heaped teaspoonful finely grated fresh horseradish. If fresh horseradish not available, use 2 teaspoonsful or more of horseradish relish. Pour into a separate dish on the side, or coat each piece of fish on the serving dish with the sauce. Serve piping hot, decorated with chopped parsley and capers. Creamed potatoes and coleslaw go well with this recipe.

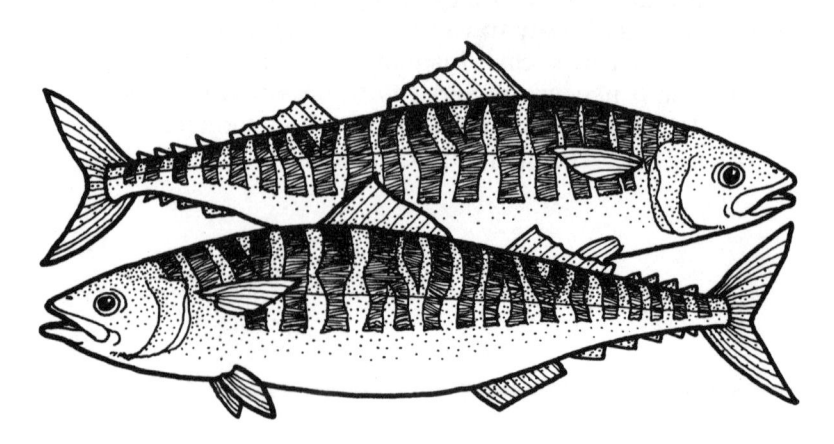

Casserole of Mackerel or Herring

One acceptable way to maintain a moderate intake of high grade proteins. Herrings are nearly fished out, but mackerel are still with us and not over-costly yet.

4 fresh mackerel or herrings
1 lb tomatoes
1 large onion
1 bay leaf
Some flour
A little butter
Brown breadcrumbs
Fresh parsley
Salt and freshly ground black pepper

Ask the fishmonger to de-scale, head and fillet the fish if you can't do so yourself. Wash and dry well, coat pieces in salted flour and set aside. Butter a shallow casserole dish. Slice tomatoes, prepare onion and slice thinly into half moons. Crush bay leaf as finely as possible. Place half of tomato and onion in bottom of dish, then sprinkle with lightly salted flour and ground pepper and half crushed bay leaf. Place in prepared fish. Cover with rest of onion, tomatoes and bay leaf, adding pepper to taste. Lastly cover with a good layer of fresh breadcrumbs, dot with butter and cook in a moderate 350°F oven for 45 minutes. Serve with creamed potatoes, to which you have added 2 generous tablespoonsful chopped parsley and, if possible, a fresh green salad on the side.

Optional variation:
Mushrooms enhance this dish. If you have some, slice 2 oz. and lay on top of the fish in dish before covering with rest of onion and so on.

Eating Chinese Style

In adjusting to The Small Island Diet, you may find home-prepared Chinese style food, with its low meat content, helpful. You can have appetising meals which are easy to cook and surprisingly inexpensive. We say Chinese 'style' because we have simplified our introductory recipes from true Chinese food. Traditional Chinese cooking can be learned from excellent cook books, though you may find them formidable enough to seek ways of simplifying them.

You will have to acquire a few basics: firstly a wok – that's a specially rounded cooking pan; a large bottle of soy sauce; and some ginger sherry. You can make this with a bottle of the cheapest British sherry and four ounces of juicy fresh ginger. Take out a glass of the sherry and in its place drop the ginger, cut into strips. Re-cork and keep for a while in the kitchen cupboard before using. Put a label on it to avoid mistakes! A few teaspoonful to any dish is enough.

Authentic Chinese food will often include bean sprouts, rice and noodles, of course. Chinese stores and some supermarkets sell bean sprouts, but your own sprouted mung beans, wheat or alfalfa are quite all right. You can use boiled wheat instead of rice; while noodles are best made at home.

Here are a couple of recipes to start you off, preceded by one for noodles.

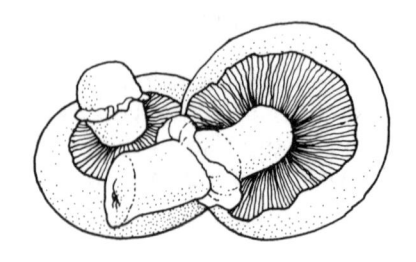

Chinese Noodles

Make your noodles fresh, just before you cook any recipe which includes them.

6 oz. strong plain flour
1 egg
1 dessertspoonful oil
Little water

Put flour into a large bowl, make a well in centre, drop in egg, oil and a very little water. Work this with the finger tips, or narrow wooden spoon, bringing flour to the middle with a circular movement. When all flour is taken up, knead well with heel of hand. Transfer to a well-floured surface, knead again and keep folding over to make a pliable dough. Cover with a cloth and leave for a while. Roll out as thinly as you can – the larger the surface, the thinner you can roll the dough. Fold into four and cut up thin strips with a very sharp knife, then into strips about 4 inches long. They should not need more than 3 or 4 minutes cooking – just drop into boiling water.

> The Diet of Affluent Malnutrition may be said to include, not only the chemicals added to foods, but those eaten regularly with or between meals. Just as increasing numbers of men and women rely on alcohol to 'keep them going' so dependence on mind-altering drugs is also rising. One in five women take them and one in ten men – about a million people on Valium alone.

Chicken and Vegetables with Noodles

An easy Chinese style recipe to begin with. A chance to get used to cooking with a wok.

> 4 tablespoonsful raw chicken, preferably breast or thigh
> 1 large onion
> 1 large carrot
> 1 small juicy green pepper
> 2 tablespoonsful white part of cabbage
> 8 oz. bean sprouts
> ½ pint hot chicken stock (page 236)
> 1 teaspoonful soy sauce
> 2 teaspoonsful cornflour
> 2 teaspoonsful ginger sherry
> 1 tablespoonful oil
> 1 tablespoonful cold water

First make the noodles (page 175) but do not cook them yet. Then put the cold water into a small bowl and work in cornflour. Add soy sauce, sherry, a little white pepper and salt, then set aside. In a small pan keep chicken stock hot. Slice chicken, carrot and cabbage into thin strips. Cut pepper in two, remove seeds and white pith, and also cut into thin strips. Set all aside.

Halve onion and cut into thin half moons. Keep separate. Pick over sprouts, throwing out any seeds. Heat oil in wok, add onion first and cook for ½ minute, moving it all the time with a wooden fork. Next add sprouts and cook for another minute. Keep moving, then add chicken and remaining vegetables and cook for another 2 minutes, tossing all the while. Pour some of the hot stock onto bowl of cornflour mixture, stir well, add to chicken and vegetables with rest of stock and cook for 2 minutes. Meanwhile have a pan of boiling water on the stove and cook noodles for 3 to 4 minutes as described. Drain them well and place on a hot serving dish. Pour over them chicken and vegetables, and decorate with chopped chives and watercress. Serve at once.

Optional variation:
Wheat or alfalfa sprouts instead of bean sprouts.

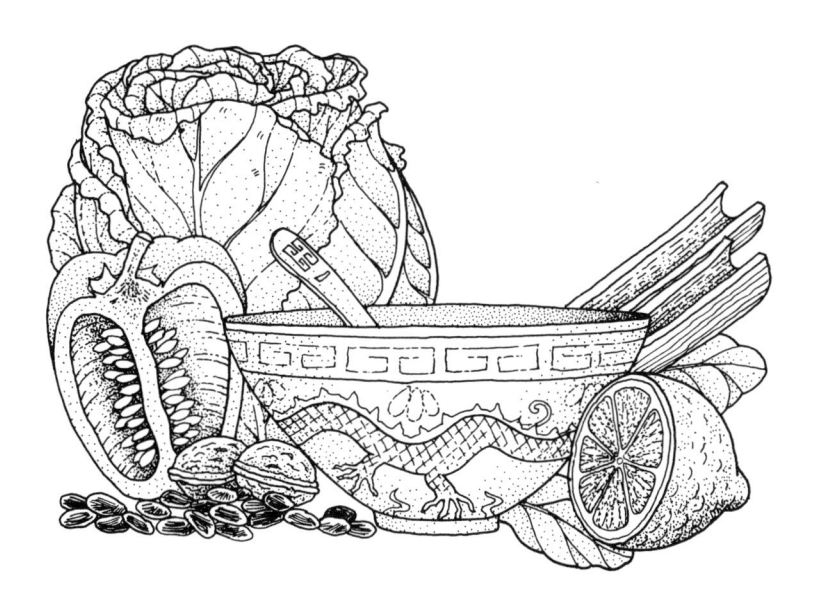

Sweet and Sour Cabbage

Like many Chinese dishes, this recipe uses ingredients not commonly eaten together.

>1 medium cabbage
>3 tomatoes
>1 carrot
>1 tablespoonful oil plus 1½ teaspoonsful
>2 tablespoonsful ginger sherry
>1 tablespoonful cornflour
>1 dessertspoonful sugar
>2 tablespoonsful vinegar – pref. cider
>2 tablespoonsful soy sauce
>½ cup chicken or vegetable stock

Take tough outer leaves from cabbage. Cut it in two and, if free from creepy-crawlies, don't wash. If you do, however, be sure to dry thoroughly in a cloth or it will spurt alarmingly in the pan. Cut into about 1½ inch squares and set aside. To make sweet and sour sauce: shred carrot, skin tomatoes, put 1½ teaspoonsful of oil in a strong pan and cook carrots and tomatoes for about 3 minutes; add vinegar, sugar and soy sauce together with ½ cup of stock in which you have blended cornflour; add to pan and bring to boil, stirring all the time until translucent; keep warm.

Put the tablespoonful of oil in wok. When hot add cabbage and cook quickly over fairly high heat for 3 minutes, moving all the time with wooden fork. Now add ginger sherry, stirring continuously to mix well in. Lower heat, pour over sweet and sour sauce, and give a final quick stir to mix well. Serve at once.

You can add a final touch by making a very thin omelette of 1 egg, well beaten with 1 tablespoonful of water with pepper and salt. Heat a little oil in fry pan, cover bottom with egg and, maintaining a low heat, set egg and turn once. Cut into thin strips and sprinkle over dish just before serving with boiled noodles.

Eating Indian Style

This great tradition has the merit of creating superb flavours in dishes with little or no meat. They don't have to be at all oily, and – contrary to common belief – rice isn't obligatory, though if you need an alternative 'tummy filler', you can substitute boiled wheat (page 232).

For delicate and appetizing curry don't use 'curry powder', but make your own blends of spice flavours for the meat or vegetables. This way you'll be able to distinguish the subtle flavours of each ingredient. What's more, you won't mask the taste of the meat or vegetable by making your curry too 'hot'. Again, contrary to general belief, the finest Indian cooking isn't necessarily 'hot' at all.

Friends introduced us to these two recipes which we hope will start you off well, but you needn't confine yourself to them. Over time, vary the ingredients and their proportions to suit your palate. To widen your variety there are plenty of fine books on exotic Indian curry dishes and their accompanying sweet and cooling condiments. In these, yogurt can come into its own for making various kinds of *raitas*, in which it is combined with vegetables or fruit, cooked or raw.

If you live in a large town you should have no difficulty in buying the spices needed for Indian cooking. Most of the 'wholefood' shops sell them and certainly any Indian food shop. But do remember that ground spices deteriorate, so unless you buy whole seeds and grind your own, don't buy too much at one time.

Vegetable Curry (Parsnip)

1 lb prepared parsnip, cut in ½ inch cubes
½ lb tomatoes
¾ pint stock
2 large onions
2 cloves garlic
2 oz. butter
2 teaspoonsful gravy mix
2 teaspoonsful reliable curry powder
2 teaspoonsful haldi powder (turmeric)
½ teaspoonful zeera powder (cummin)
½ teaspoonful dhania powder (coriander)
¼ teaspoonful paprika
Some zeera seeds
Some fennel seeds
Some dhania seeds
A few cardamon pods
1 teaspoonful salt

Melt butter in a strong deep pan. Skin and cut up tomatoes, prepare onion and cut finely into half moons. Cook in butter with tomatoes, crushed garlic and all the spices until onions are soft. Add stock and gravy mix and cubed parsnip.
Simmer gently for about 30 minutes or until parsnip is firm but tender. Tastes better re-heated next day, as all curries do!
If you like, serve with spinach to which you have added butter and some methi powder to your taste.
Use plenty of condiments on the side.
Serve with a dhal – recipe opposite.

Dhal

2 teacupsful cooked sieved beans
1 medium onion
1 oz. butter
1 clove garlic
1 teaspoonful ginger
¼-½ teaspoonful tabasco
½ pint stock
1 teaspoonful salt

Cook onion and garlic in butter, add stock, sieved beans and rest of ingredients then mix thoroughly to combine flavours.

> We use a pepper mill to grind our spices, but they can be crushed in a pestle and mortar. The flavour of freshly ground spices are far superior to the bought ground variety which seem to deteriorate very quickly, losing their oils and aroma.

Meat Curry

1 lb lean mutton or beef
2 large onions
4 bay leaves
Seeds from 5 cardamon pods
½ teaspoonful freshly ground black pepper
½ teaspoonful ground mace (nutmeg will do at a pinch)
½ teaspoonful ground cinnamon
½ teaspoonful ground ginger
¼ teaspoonful cloves
4 tablespoonsful oil
Meat or vegetable stock (page 236)
Crushed garlic clove if liked
Level teaspoonful salt

Prepare onions and cut up thinly into half moons. Brown in oil in strong, deep pan. Cut up meat into thin pieces about 1 inch long. Add to onions and brown well. Add all spices, stirring constantly and cook for a few minutes. Cover with stock, add salt and simmer gently with lid on for 40 minutes or so. Serve with boiled wheat (page 232). About 10 minutes before end of cooking time stir in to the wheat 2 oz. of skinned almonds, halved and cut lengthways once more, 2 oz. washed sultanas and 1 teaspoonful ground mace.

Eating Italian Style

If you were to ask what Italian food is doing in a book on predominantly British food, we'd say that our island of merchant adventurers has traditionally relished the ideas on eating they introduced, and that the low meat, high herb character of many Italian dishes eminently fits the criteria of our Diet for A Small Island. What's more we *like* Italian food!

We have modified recipes of the country, however, not only to make the most of British ingredients, but also to reduce the oil content. The result is variety, flavour, nourishment and economy in recipes which you may find especially helpful for cutting down on meat, since the tomato, garlic and herb flavours go some way to bridging the gap. Finally, to any native readers we may possibly offend we humbly say 'Scusi'.

A farm animal or bird, on average, must eat about eight pounds of grain and vegetable protein to produce one pound for us to eat as meat, milk and eggs. Comparative figures for different foods are: grain-fed beef 21 lb; pork 8 lb; poultry 5½ lb; milk and eggs 4½ lb. An acre of cereals can produce five times more protein than one acre running livestock; peas and beans ten times more, and leafy vegetables 15 times more.

Pizza Pie

This amount will make a large pizza for four. Alternatively you can divide it into four portions and make different toppings for each. The topping described is one of our favourites, but there are many others to choose from, depending on whether or not you are a strict vegetarian.

For the dough:–
1 lb wholemeal, sieved wholemeal or 81% flour
½ oz. yeast
¼ pint warm milk (about)
3 eggs
2 oz. butter
1 teaspoonful sugar
1 teaspoonful salt

Mix flour and salt in warm basin. Cream yeast with sugar and add warm milk in which you have melted butter. Beat eggs and mix into yeast mixture. Work thoroughly into flour, making sure all flour is taken up and dough is smooth. Set to rise for 30 to 40 minutes. Meanwhile make the following topping. Turn out pizza dough on to a floured surface, knead slightly and roll into a round or rounds about ½ inch or less thick. Use a flan ring to keep dough in position if you like. Cook at 400°F for 10 minutes.

For the topping:–
1 portion smoked Mackerel
2 oz. strong Cheddar cheese
1 lb ripe tomatoes or 1 lb jar preserved tomatoes
1 medium onion
1 clove garlic
2 teaspoonsful dried sweet basil or fresh rosemary or origano or mixture
2 teaspoonsful capers
1 tablespoonful oil
Salt and freshly ground black pepper

Slice onion thinly and melt down in oil. Skin tomatoes, chop, then cook in a strong pan until soft. Press through a sieve to remove seeds. Put back into pan with crushed garlic and reduce the moisture. The tomato should be thick but pourable. If using bottled tomatoes, drain juice and set aside for soup. Press pulp through a sieve into a pan and reduce with garlic as before. Season with salt and pepper. Take pizza from oven, spread tomato purée over dough, then spread onion, 1 teaspoonful of herbs and half the cheese. Flake mackerel and place evenly over this. Lastly sprinkle rest of cheese, capers and rest of herbs on top. Return to oven for further 15 minutes at 300°F; the flavours will then have combined and the cheese melted. Serve immediately if possible, with a mixed tossed green salad.

Optional Variations:
Leave out the fish and cook ½ lb of sliced mushrooms in some red wine. Use strips of cooked ham or streaky bacon, halves of pickled walnuts, black olives ... great scope for imagination!

Home-Made Pasta

Tastier and cheaper than what you buy, but be prepared for a spot of hard work. If you don't mind that, you'll find the results really satisfying. Make a batch to use fresh or dry it to store for another time. Serve it with any recipe which needs a pasta base.

1 lb sieved wholemeal or
81% or unbleached white flour
3 lightly beaten eggs
2 teaspoonsful salt
3 or 4 tablespoonsful water

Put flour and salt in a large bowl, mix together, make a well in the centre, pour in egg and water, then work into flour with the fingers of one hand. A little more water may be needed if you use sieved wholemeal flour. When all the flour has been taken up, knead well – this is where the hard work comes in – the dough should be stiff and must be kneaded for 10 minutes until an even texture.
Flour a large surface, pull off a piece of dough, keeping rest covered with a damp cloth to avoid drying out. Roll out into a square, turning on well floured surface often until very thin. Practice will make perfect! Now cut this into thin ¼ inch strips, or wider strips if making lasagne, by folding in three and cutting with a very sharp knife. Lay out on a clean teatowel to dry.
Continue in this way until all the dough is used. Make any shapes you like. Experiment. Cook it in the usual way for pasta but make sure the water is boiling fast. You can use it fresh, but if you want to keep it, dry it in a very cool oven for a few hours, or leave out on the tea towels, covered, in a warm kitchen overnight. Store in an airtight container.

Potato Gnocchi

Another pasta recipe – this one made from left-over boiled potatoes. Easy to make, and of course cheaper than bought gnocchi – if you can find any in Britain – it has its very own flavour and texture.

1 lb boiled potatoes
4 oz. flour (81% or unbleached white)
1 egg
Little freshly grated nutmeg
Salt and pepper

Sieve cooked potato into bowl, add nutmeg, pepper, salt, flour and lightly beaten egg. Mix very well together into a workable dough. Have plenty of flour on a board and on your hands, and form into small balls. Keep on floured surface until all are made, then flatten each one with the back of a fork. Have a large pan of boiling salted water ready. Drop into it a dozen of the gnocchi at a time. Keep the water boiling and wait for them to rise to the top of the water. When they do, it shows they are ready, so remove with a slotted spoon, place on a heated plate and keep warm. Repeat until all are cooked. They're delicious served with melted butter and lots of chopped parsley or garlic butter or a liberal amount of grated strong cheese. You should also enjoy them in the pasta sauce (page 191), even more perhaps if you add meat balls (page 169).

China, India and Italy are, of course, not the only countries whose ways of eating correspond with The Small Island Diet. You can add still more variety and adventure by including dishes adapted from those of other countries bordering the Mediterranean, from the near, middle and far East, from Africa, South America and the Caribbean. Recipe books of exotic foods abound: all you must do is discriminate between elitist, over-rich, gourmet dishes and the simple but admirable, traditional dishes of ordinary folk.

Forcemeat

To use with chicken, rabbit or game dishes.

½ lb breadcrumbs
1 oz. butter
¼ lb minced ham or bacon pieces
1 tablespoonful chopped parsley
1 teaspoonful chopped lemon balm
½ teaspoonful thyme
1 small egg
Salt and pepper

Work butter into breadcrumbs, add rest of ingredients and mix well before adding beaten egg. If not moist enough add a little milk. Can be rolled into balls if required.

Chestnut Stuffing

Try this popular recipe in place of the usual forcemeat or sausage meat stuffing next time you have poultry. Note its low-fat content!

2 lb prepared chestnuts
2 beaten eggs
2 oz. butter
1 teacupful chopped onion
1 teacupful chopped celery or grated celeriac
2 tablespoonsful chopped fresh parsley
6 teacupsful stale breadcrumbs
3 teacupsful grated cooking apples
Salt and pepper

Prepare chestnuts as recommended below. Cook in a little stock for about 20 minutes. Drain and chop into small pieces. Put butter in large saucepan and when melted cook for a few minutes celery (or celeriac), onion and parsley until onion is soft. Keep moving with wooden fork. Remove from heat and, when cool, stir in rest of ingredients except eggs. Beat these and fold into mixture to combine thoroughly. This amount will stuff a 10 to 12 lb turkey. Use half quantities for chicken.

To Shell Chestnuts
Slit nuts with a cross on the flat side. If already using the oven, place them on a tray and cook for 20 minutes or so at 350°F until shells curl back. If not, slit as before, place in large pan of boiling water, boil for 10 minutes. Take nuts out one at a time. They peel very easily this way.

Thick Cheese Sauce

1 pint milk
¼ lb tasty cheese
2 tablespoonsful white flour
1 teaspoonful dry mustard
Salt and pepper to taste

Combine flour, mustard, salt and pepper in pan. Grate cheese. Add a little of the milk at a time to make a smooth paste. Then add rest of milk until mixed in smoothly. Cook over moderate heat until thick, stirring all the time – about 5 minutes. Combine grated cheese last and stir over low heat until melted.
If you have a blender, put milk and grated cheese in first, then dry ingredients and blend for ½ minute. Pour into pan and over moderate heat stir continually until cooked and thick.

Basic White Sauce

A sauce is an important adjunct to very many dishes. To a basic white sauce you can add many flavourings – such as herbs, cheese, egg, mustard, capers and so on. Use it to combine leftover meat, fish or vegetables for other dishes. You can also add sweet flavourings and use it for puddings. In this simple sauce no fat is used, but to make it richer, for different dishes where a richer sauce is called for, add ½-1oz. butter – work into the sauce until melted after cooking.

1 pint milk (about)
2 tablespoonsful white flour

Work a little milk into the flour to make a smooth paste. Warm rest of milk, add gradually stirring all the time over a gentle heat until thoroughly combined. Bring to boil and cook for five minutes. The amount of milk will depend on the thickness of the sauce required.

Pasta Sauce

The full bodied flavour of our favourite sauce is ideal, not only for pasta, but with meat balls (page 169), pancakes (page 125) or vegetable marrow and pumpkin.

1 lb ripe tomatoes
1 large onion
¼ lb mushrooms
1 tablespoonful Worcestershire sauce or
2 tablespoonsful tomato ketchup (page 239)
¼ pint red wine or stock
2 tablespoonsful oil
1 bay leaf
1 large clove garlic
1 teaspoonful fresh chopped lemon balm
1 teaspoonful fresh chopped rosemary
Salt and freshly ground black pepper

Skin tomatoes and chop, slice onion thinly, slice mushrooms thinly. Put oil in heavy based pan, cook onion for a few minutes, add tomatoes, mushrooms, bay leaf, crushed garlic, herbs, seasoning and wine or stock, then stir well. Simmer very gently for about 30 minutes, then, just before serving, add Worcestershire sauce or tomato ketchup.

To Clarify Fat

Save the pieces of fat from any meat. Put into a pan with boiling water and simmer gently for about 1 hour. Strain into a bowl. When cold run a sharp knife round the bowl, take off the disc of fat carefully, scrape off any residue from the underside. Boil fat once more in a strong pan until the surface is still, when any further moisture will have evaporated. Pour into a strong container to cool. Pure beef dripping makes very good savoury pastry, fruit cakes and gingerbread.

7
DESSERTS, PUDDINGS AND CAKES

You may be disappointed not to find more cake and pudding recipes in this chapter. We are sorry, but it is intentional. Those we have given are basic recipes chiefly, onto which you can build, or which you can adapt to enlarge your repertoire of low-fat and low-sugar treats. For, let's face it, we are talking about treats, even though they have become a daily – or three times daily – habit. If you are serious about health, your own and your family's, you have to work towards skipping the 'sweet' course for at least one meal a day, and at other meals substituting raw or cooked fruit for puddings, pies, trifles and so on. We are not suggesting 'Ban the cake' banners or buttons, just saying 'Cool it.'

Besides having less sugar and fat than usual, many of our recipes advise wholemeal flour, but knowing that this can present adaptation difficulties, we also suggest *unbleached* white flour to help you through the transition. You may have to hunt around for it, but it will be worth the trouble.

One more word about sugar. Purists may be horrified to see we specify white sugar in many of our recipes. Let them rant and rave! What does the harm is an excess of *total* sugars of all kinds. Sucrose – that's cane sugar – may be more harmful than other kinds, but you are fooling yourself if you believe that eating it brown will save you from damnation! Most brown sugar is just white sugar with the molasses put back – at extra cost to the consumer. We don't see the point of spoiling recipes with subtle flavours by masking them with the taste of molasses, pleasant though it may be.

Finally, essences as flavourings. Sadly, most of the little bottles are full of chemical substitutes. You *can* buy the real thing, however, and suppliers are given in the Ideas for Action Section.

Mellow Fruitfulness

Although much of our fruit grown in Britain is unsurpassed when eaten raw – such as strawberries, raspberries, loganberries and some varieties of apples, pears and plums – our climate lacks the sunshine which most fruits need for an abundance of natural sugar. Sadly, no amount of sugar added to them while raw can disguise their tartness. We must cook them so that the cellulose breaks down and allows the added sugar – or honey – to neutralise their natural acids.

This is where the trouble begins. Too many of us add too much sugar at the wrong time; we plunge the fruit into too much water and cook it for far too long. As a result, flavour is spoiled; much of what remains is transferred to the water – and the excessive, wishy-washy juice is often thrown away; nourishment – especially vitamins – is lost, and fuel is wasted.

The remedy is simple. Part-cook gently before adding sugar or honey. Add water only as may be necessary to supplement the juices so released. Continue cooking for just as long as the fruit needs to 'melt' and absorb the sweetness. The whole takes only a few minutes and leaves you with no unwanted liquid. Here are a few recipes by way of example.

To sweeten fresh fruit salads, whether with sugar or honey, make a syrup with the juiciest of the fruits and pour a little at a time over the layers. Serve with yogurt or the sauce on page 205 instead of cream.

Stewed Plums

Plums
Sugar or honey to taste

Wash plums and stone them carefully. Place in strong pan over gentle heat with lid on until juice begins to run. This takes just a few minutes. Add sugar or honey and cook gently without lid until melted – about 5 minutes.

Stewed Rhubarb

About 1 lb rhubarb
1 tablespoonful water
Sugar or honey to taste

Wash and wipe rhubarb. Cut into inch-long pieces. Place in strong pan with the water over gentle heat with lid on until juice begins to run – a few minutes. Add sugar or honey and cook gently until each piece is melted yet remains whole – about 5 minutes.

Every year, Britain's shops are inundated with French apples – pithy and almost tasteless, yet oddly named 'Golden Delicious'. Meanwhile crisp, sweet British apples rot by the million, for under the weird rules of the EEC most of our proven, old-fashioned varieties are now banned from sale.

Special Cooked Apple

About 1 lb eating apples
1 oz. butter
1 tablespoonful sugar
½ teaspoonful cinnamon

Wash and dry apples. Cut into 4, core, and cut once more. (It shouldn't be necessary to peel them if organically grown. If using ordinary shop apples however peeling is advisable to remove absorbed poisonous sprays.) Put butter into strong wide pan or fry pan and melt over medium heat. Place apples in butter and cook until golden, turning once. Once the natural sugar comes out of the fruit, take special care not to burn them. Spoon carefully into fireproof serving dish. Mix sugar and cinnamon together and sprinkle over top. Place under a low grill for a few minutes to crispen but not burn; or if you have the oven going, place dish on low shelf for about 10 minutes.

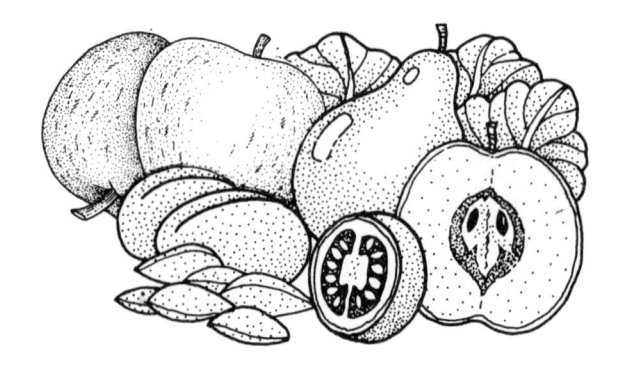

Fruit Delight

Another favourite cold sweet which will, if needs be, make use of damaged and second grade fruit.

*1½ lb strawberries or raspberries
or a mixture of both
4 oz. sugar – or more if suffering
withdrawal symptoms!
1 pint water
4 flat tablespoonsful cornflour
Cream, yogurt, custard
or sweet creamy sauce (page 205)*

Pick over fruit and wash if necessary. Cook in ½ pint water until soft – a few minutes only. Pour through sieve into another pan and press fruit through sieve until only seeds remain. Add sugar and stir until dissolved. Take a small amount of water from the remaining ½ pint and mix cornflour to a smooth paste. Gradually add rest of water to this and, stirring all the time, add to fruit juice in pan. Slowly bring to boil over low heat and cook, stirring continuously, for about 8 minutes. Pour into a warm glass dish. When quite cold serve with the cream or other suggestions.

No need to add extra sugar to dried fruit, such as apricots, peaches, prunes and figs. Just wash well and pour on boiling water to cover, then leave to plump up. No further cooking is needed.

If you set yourself a 'sugar ration', there's no better way to use it than to make our own British fruits palatable.

Mixed Fruit Dessert

Cottage cheese in an unusual marriage with fruit. On a self-sufficient smallholding, every ingredient could be home produced – as in many of our recipes. Imperfect fruit is no problem.

4 oz. curd or cottage cheese
2 tablespoonsful milk
1 tablespoonful honey or sugar
1 tablespoonful chopped nuts
1 apple
1 pear
Some cherries or raspberries

Pass cheese through a sieve, mix with milk and sugar. Gently fold in the cut-up fruit. Serve at once in individual dishes, decorated with nuts.

Optional Variations:
Instead of fruit given above try 4 tablespoonsful of bottled blackcurrants or gooseberries, well drained. Or a mixture of any fruit to hand.

Pears in Elderberry Wine

Here's a country recipe for making a delicious sweet from those old-fashioned flavourless, hard pears. If you have such a tree, try this before using the axe ...

Halve, peel and core some pears. Warm some honey in a large heavy pan and place pears, cut side down. Very gently, over low heat with lid on, cook for about 10 minutes. Add a teacupful or more of elderberry wine, depending on how many pears, and cook fast without the lid until the wine is reduced by half. Allow to cool in pan. Serve with yoghurt, cream or sauce (page 205).

Blackcurrant Ice

Although this is irresistible on hot days with yogurt, cream or sauce (page 205), you'll also find it invaluable for using up the over-ripe fruit, inevitable in any time of glut. Highly nourishing, of course.

½ lb fresh blackcurrants
½ pint water
3 tablespoonsful honey

Make a syrup with honey and water. When cool, put half syrup, half blackcurrants in blender and run until fruit is pulped. Pour into bowl. Repeat with other half. Mix thoroughly with first lot of fruit, pour into ice trays and freeze.

Honey can be used in place of sugar in cakes and sweets, though you'd do best to hunt around for a source of reasonably priced honey, possibly by buying bulk. Remember that it contains water, whereas sugar doesn't, so adjust recipes accordingly. Also it burns more easily, so bake in a cooler oven and keep a watchful eye on whatever you're baking. One more point: it will tend to curdle milk if cooked at the same time, so when using honey in custard or sauce, add it after cooking. And don't forget that you can use honey to sweeten fresh fruit salads and cooked fruit.

Summer Trifle

The scope for different trifles is almost limitless and they needn't be over-rich. This is one of our favourites.

1-1½ lb raspberries or strawberries
Little honey or sugar
Sponge cake (page 215)
4 tablespoonsful sherry or brandy
1 pint milk
2 eggs
3 teaspoonsful cornflour (heaped)
1 tablespoonful fine vanilla sugar

Put fruit into a strong pan, melt down until juice is released. Sprinkle over a little sugar or honey and cook for just a few minutes. Allow to cool, mix in sherry or brandy and pour through a sieve into a suitable glass dish. Cover with pieces of cake. Then spread fruit from the sieve evenly over the cake. Cover with more cake and press down. Put cornflour in a bowl with a little milk and vanilla sugar then work to a smooth consistency. Heat milk. In a bowl beat eggs until fluffy and add to cornflour mixture. Pour over hot milk stirring all the time. Pour through a sieve into pan and cook over gentle heat until thick. Leave in pan to cool, covered with a piece of wet greaseproof paper to stop a skin forming. When cool pour over fruit and cake. Let stand till next day. Beat up some cream. Decorate top with cream, fresh raspberries or strawberries and flaked almonds.

A recent survey found that over 60 per cent of five-year-old children had decayed milk teeth, and that school-leavers had nearly a third of their teeth either decayed or filled. Only three per cent of them had no signs of dental decay. Sugar abuse is the prime cause of dental decay.

Plum Surprise

Gluts – when shop prices tumble and garden produce threatens to overwhelm you – should be times for glee not groans. Take plums for example. Grumbles of 'Not plums again!' can easily be stifled with recipes such as this.

About 1 lb plums, bottled or stewed
3 eggs
¾ pint milk
3½ tablespoonsful sugar
2 tablespoonsful cornflour
1 teaspoonful almond essence
1 oz. butter

You'll need an 8 inch pie dish. Drain juice from fruit. Make a pastry cream as follows: Separate egg whites from yolks. Put egg whites into large dry bowl with pinch salt. Beat egg yolks and add milk to them. Put cornflour in pan and mix to a smooth consistency with some of the egg/milk mixture, then gradually add more until all mixed together. Place over medium heat and, stirring all the time, cook until thick. After moving from heat add ½ tablespoonful sugar, the butter and essence. Beat well with wooden spoon until all combined. Pour into pie dish and smooth over evenly. Cover this pastry cream all over with halves of fruit.

Make *meringue* with the egg whites as follows: Beat them until dry and stiff. Add 2 tablespoonsful sugar – it should be granulated – one tablespoonful at a time, beating well in. Then fold in the third tablespoonful. Cover the fruit with this *meringue*, making sure that there are no gaps at the edge of the dish. Peak up with flat of a knife. Cook in cool oven until crisp and golden – at least 1 hour. Serve while still warm, preferably with cream.

Flan Pastry

Less rich than is customary, this recipe is the basis for the flan recipe which follows and any open fruit flans you may make.

½ lb flour – 81% or sieved wholemeal
2 oz. butter and 2 oz. lard
or 4 oz. vegetable fat or margarine
1 tablespoonful fine sugar
Yolk of 1 egg
¼ teaspoonful salt
Little water

Mix flour and salt in a bowl. Work in fat until like breadcrumbs. Mix in sugar and lastly work egg yolk well into mixture and add a little water if necessary to make it into a workable dough. Let it stand for a while before using.

> *If you have a blender, don't buy expensive caster sugar. Just put granulated sugar in the grinder attachment and run for a few seconds – perfect for sponge cakes. Keep some in a jar with vanilla pods for flavouring when needed.*

Cottage Cheese and Honey Flan

Anyone can make and enjoy this flan, but few so well as a self-supporter on a small farm with his own cheese, eggs and honey. As it is something of a treat, it's best served after a simple first course such as mixed salad, for a little goes a long way.

½ lb flan pastry (opposite)
½ lb cottage cheese
3 oz. honey
2 eggs
Some cinnamon or nutmeg if liked

Warm honey in a large bowl over hot water. Sieve cheese onto warmed honey and mix thoroughly. Add well beaten eggs. Line an 8 inch flan ring with the pastry. Pour in cottage cheese mixture, sprinkle with cinnamon or nutmeg and bake in moderate oven at 350°F on middle shelf for 35 minutes – until set and attractively golden.
If any pastry over, roll out and cut into shapes, put on a greased baking sheet and cook for about 10 minutes for use later with stewed fruit.

Real Custard

In Mrs. Beaton's day, custard was always made with eggs. Only when cheap cornflour substitutes came on the market did it become necessary to add the prefix 'egg' to distinguish the real thing – extra delicious and nourishing, but now almost forgotten. This is how we make it.

½ pint milk
1 egg
2 teaspoonsful sugar
1 rounded teaspoonful white flour
A few drops of vanilla essence

Optional variations:
2 teaspoonsful honey
1 rounded teaspoonful custard powder
Vanilla pods

Put the flour or custard powder in a pan. Add a little of the milk and mix to a smooth paste. Beat egg. Add with rest of milk, slowly stirring all the time. Cook over low heat, stirring continuously, until it thickens. Do not boil. Remove from heat and stir in sugar or honey. Add vanilla essence or – better still – be prepared and instead of plain sugar use some which has stood for at least a month with a vanilla pod in a sealed jar.

When making custard for a pudding which is already sweet, use only 1 teaspoonful of sugar or honey to ½ pint. Remember to blend in honey after cooking to prevent it curdling.

Sweet Creamy Sauce

For fruit salad or stewed fruit this 'instant' sauce makes a welcome change from custard or cream. It is delicious, nutritious and low in fat. If you happen to keep goats or a house cow, it will help to make use of surplus milk.

¼ lb cottage or curd cheese
1 small egg
3 tablespoonsful top of milk
1 dessertspoonful vanilla sugar (below)

Simply put all in blender for ½ minute. You can make it without the egg and you can use yogurt instead of milk if you wish.

Vanilla Sugar

Cut up two or three vanilla pods and place in a 1lb jar of sugar, shake occasionally. Replace sugar and vanilla pods when necessary. You can use any pod that you have cooked in milk for custard and so on. Just wash and dry well, and put back with the sugar.

Medieval Parsnip Pie

Our ancestors knew what they were up to when they used parsnips in this unusual way. Keep the pie's chief ingredient a secret – and keep guests or family guessing a long while! Extra welcome in winter in fresh fruit scarcity.

1 lb cooked parsnips
3 egg yolks
2 egg whites
4 tablespoonsful honey
¼ teaspoonful ground ginger
¼ teaspoonful powdered mace (preferably) or nutmeg
½ teaspoonful cinnamon

Line a 9-inch shallow dish with flan pastry (page 202), saving some for latticework strips. Prick base and partially bake in 350°F oven. Mash and sieve parsnips, beat egg yolks, then, with honey and spices, combine with parsnips. In a dry clean bowl beat egg whites thoroughly but not too dry. Fold into parsnip mixture. Pour mixture into pastry case and decorate in latticework with pastry strips. Return to oven for 30 to 35 minutes to set and brown latticework. Eat while still warm with fresh or soured cream.

Six slices of bread, 18 lumps of sugar, 1 lb of potatoes, ¾ pint of milk and two pints of beer all have about the same energy value; and each provides the energy for a four mile walk (at 4 m.p.h.), an hour's tennis or gardening and 2 hours D.I.Y. house repairs. Over time, unused energy is deposited round the body as fat.

Baked Fruity Batter

Always popular, this not-too-sweet pudding is one of a number of ways to make good use of windfalls and imperfect fruits.

6 oz. flour, 81% or unbleached white
½ pint milk, fresh or sour
2 eggs
1 tablespoonful honey or vanilla sugar (page 205)
1 teaspoonful baking powder
Pinch salt
1 lb eating apples (red ones look more enticing) or plums
Extra sugar
Some cinnamon

If you have a blender make batter in it by putting eggs, milk, sugar, salt and baking powder in first, flour last. Blend for ½ minute, then with spatula push down any unmixed flour, then blend for another ½ minute. Stand for 1 hour. Just before using blend for a few seconds. Quarter the apples and core, cut once again. Set aside. Heat a well-buttered 10 inch shallow oven-to-table dish in 400°F oven. When hot – about 5 minutes – pour in batter, place prepared apples or, if using plums, stone them and carefully place, cut surface down, into batter. Cook middle shelf for 20 minutes. Remove from oven and generously sprinkle with sugar; dust with cinnamon if liked. Return to oven for 10 minutes more or until batter is cooked. Serve at once.

Plum Layer Pudding

Ideal for hearty appetites, this pudding tastes rich even though it's not. Something to do with the alternate layers of fruit and 'cakiness'.

Some plums or damsons
½ lb wholemeal flour
3 oz. butter, margarine or vegetable fat
3 oz. brown sugar
Extra sugar if needed
1 or 2 teaspoonsful mixed spice
1 teaspoonful baking powder
Good pinch salt

Mix salt, baking powder and spices into flour. Rub or fork the fat into the flour as for pastry, add the sugar and mix well. Butter very well a 7 inch soufflé dish. Sprinkle a layer of flour mixture over bottom of dish. Stone fruit and cover flour mixture. Sprinkle a little extra sugar over the fruit if not very sweet. Continue in layers, finishing with flour mixture. Dot with butter and cook in slow oven for about 1 hour 30 mins and the top is crunchy. Let it stand for 15 minutes before serving. Can be eaten hot or cold. Serve with cream or custard or any favourite sauce.

Make more pastry crumbs than one recipe needs. Keep them in a covered container in the fridge or cool place. You can use them for a quick crumble with added sugar to make a sweet from any left-over fruit.

DESSERTS, PUDDINGS AND CAKES

Spiced Apple Cake

Here we have just one delicious way you can use the spiced apple preserve on page 242. Eat it hot as a pudding with custard or cream, or cold as cake.

8 oz. 85% wholemeal flour
2 oz. sugar or 1 tablespoonful honey or syrup
2 tablespoonsful honey or syrup
4 oz. butter, margarine or vegetable fat
1 egg
2 teaspoonsful baking powder
6 tablespoonsful spiced apple
A little milk
Salt

Mix well together flour, baking powder and salt. Work fat into mixture until the consistency of breadcrumbs. Make a well in the centre, beat egg and pour in. Roughly cut up spiced apple and add 4 tablespoonsful then sugar or 1 tablespoonful honey or 1 tablespoonful syrup. Rinse out last of egg with the milk and add to mixture. This should be fairly moist. If not add more milk. Mix thoroughly. Grease well a 9 inch by 1½ inch dish. Spread remaining 2 tablespoonsful of honey or syrup in bottom. Pour in mixture. Decorate with remaining spiced apple. Bake in moderate 350°F oven on middle shelf for about 30-45 mins or until a knife comes out clean when testing.

Fruit Crumble

The ever-popular standby – basic, quick and easy. With the wonderful variety of wild and cultivated fruits of Britain, freshly gathered or naturally stored, monotony would be inexcusable.

4 oz. wholemeal flour
2 oz. brown or white sugar
Pinch salt
1½ oz. butter, margarine or vegetable cooking fat
Some stewed fruit

Work butter into flour as for pastry, add sugar and mix well. Put stewed fruit in bottom of a dish and sprinkle crumble mixture on top. Cook in middle of moderate oven for 20 minutes – until nicely browned. Serve with cream or custard (page 204).

Wholemeal Shortcrust Pastry

For all recipes using pastry, such as sweet or savoury pies.

8 oz. wholemeal flour
3½ oz. vegetable fat or 4 oz. margarine
½ teaspoonful baking powder
¼ teaspoonful salt
Water to mix

Mix baking powder and salt with flour and work in fat. Add 3 tablespoonsful water and work into mixture with a fork – more water may be needed to make a soft dough. Let it stand for 30 minutes to an hour before making.

Optional variation:
Add 1 tablespoonful fine sugar.

Quick Sponge Topping

For any cooked fruit, this spongey crust can be made in minutes. The wholemeal flour gives it a distinctive, nutty flavour and a really crunchy top.

4 oz. wholemeal flour
1½ oz. vegetable cooking fat
2 oz. fine sugar
1 egg
1 tablespoonful milk
Pinch salt

Beat sugar, fat, eggs and salt together until all completely combined. Fold in flour gradually with milk. Smooth carefully over hot fruit in a 7 inch shallow pie dish. Cook for 15 minutes in 400°F oven. Serve if desired with cream, custard (page 204), or sweet creamy sauce (page 205).

Optional variations:
½ teaspoonful favourite spice
Few drops vanilla or almond essence

There is no need to buy expensive brown sugar. Make your own! Have a large bowl, a wooden spoon, 1 lb of granulated white sugar and some molasses.

Depending on how dark you like your sugar, at first add only 1 tablespoonful molasses and work this into the sugar until all is taken up. Add more molasses if a very dark sugar is required, or add more sugar if you want it lighter. Anyway you can experiment. There are very few, if any, brown sugars on the market where the molasses has not been added after the sugar has been refined. So why pay twice as much for something you can do at home? But remember, whether you use refined white or brown sugars or honey in your diet, they all finish up as glucose in your bloodstream.

Frumenty (Wheat Pudding)

This traditional old country dish can be eaten at any time of the day – though most people prefer to leave out the brandy for breakfast! It is a nutritious, well-balanced way of satisfying hearty appetites, especially in winter.

1 teacupful wheat grain
2 teacupsful milk
1 egg
2 oz. raisins or sultanas
Some honey or sugar
Cinnamon to taste
Brandy if liked

Boil wheat in strong medium pan (page 232). Soak fruit in a little hot water. Measure 2 teacupsful of hot milk onto the cooked wheat and simmer gently until milk is almost all absorbed – about 15 minutes. Remove from heat. Drain fruit through a sieve and shake to remove excess water. Add to wheat with a tablespoon of honey or sugar and cinnamon to taste and, if you have it, 2 tablespoonsful brandy. Lastly add beaten egg. Combine well. Return to very gentle heat until thickened. Serve hot.

No need to finish every meal with something sweet. When you do, remember that cake can take the place of pudding. If pudding has been the rule, limit it to once a day at first and then serve it even less often, substituting fruit – preferably fresh.

DESSERTS, PUDDINGS AND CAKES

Plain Sponge Cake

Contrary to conventional wisdom you *can* make a sponge with wholemeal flour. Try your hand with this basic recipe – if you don't succeed first time, substitute unbleached white flour until you've regained your nerve! You can add any flavour to this recipe, but not dried fruit.

½ lb wholemeal, sieved, 81%
or unbleached white flour
4 oz. margarine
3 oz. fine sugar
2 eggs (1 if pushed)
¼ pint warm milk more or less
2 teaspoonsful baking powder
Pinch salt

Mix flour, baking powder and salt together thoroughly. Beat margarine and sugar until fluffy. Beat eggs, work into the margarine and sugar adding flour in tablespoonsful a little at a time with the milk, working in each addition gently to combine all very well. Oil an 8 x 2 inch sandwich tin and line base with buttered paper cut to size. Pour mixture into prepared and warmed tin. Bake in pre-heated 350°F oven until golden and set – 30 to 45 minutes. Test with knife. Leave in the tin for 10 minutes before turning onto a stand to cool.
Cuts better after a day.

To cut down drastically on the sugar used in all cakes you make, use up to half the amount specified in the usual recipes. This specially applies when making rich fruit cake or one with dates, for there is plenty of natural sugar in the fruit already.

Eggless Spice Cake

Although this cake uses less of almost everything, it tastes good, stays moist and is nutritious. We find it especially handy when we're short of eggs. You can turn it into a pudding by cutting into slices and either toasting or heating in oven to serve with or without custard. It keeps well.

¾ lb wholemeal or 81% flour
(½ white ½ wholemeal if liked)
6 oz. margarine, butter or vegetable fat
4 oz. mixed fruit – sultanas or raisins
4 tablespoonsful of apple sauce
or stewed apples
3 oz. sugar
2 tablespoonsful molasses
3 teaspoonsful baking powder
2 teaspoonsful mixed spice, ginger or cinnamon
¼ teaspoonful salt
Little milk

Put flour, salt, spices and baking powder into large bowl and combine thoroughly. Work fat into flour. Mix in dried fruit and sugar. Make a well in centre, put in molasses and apple, mix thoroughly. If too stiff add a little milk. Line a 7 inch cake tin with greased paper.
Pour in mixture. Bake in 350°F oven until a knife inserted comes out clean – about 45 minutes to 1 hour. Leave in tin to cool.

Sponge Cake Without Fat

An easily made, no-fat, low-sugar sponge mixture with many uses. It is just the cake you need to appease young children. Cut it into fingers and it is handy to serve with stewed fruit. And for trifles it is ideal – far preferable to expensive, bought trifle sponges which may contain preservative and colouring.

2 eggs
2 oz. fine vanilla sugar (page 205)
4 oz. unbleached white flour
¼ teaspoonful baking powder
1 tablespoonful warm water

Sift baking powder into flour. Break eggs into bowl and whip for 2 or 3 minutes. Add sugar and whip again until thick and light in colour. Add water, stir flour in carefully. Cook in 8½ inch sandwich tin for 15 minutes or 9 x 12 inch Swiss roll tin for 10-11 minutes at 400°F oven middle shelf. Leave in tin for a few minutes before turning out to cool.

Try to avoid icing cakes and making butter icings and fillings. For a crunchy top to a sponge cake just scatter granulated sugar over the top at the last moment before baking. Another way to give cakes a festive look is to glaze them with a little honey while still hot. Simplest of all is a light dusting with powdered sugar when the cake is cold!

Cheese Cake

If this conjures up guilt thoughts of over-rich, over-sweet indulgence, relax, for help is on the way. With this recipe you can make an economical cheese cake with only a fraction of the fat and sugar in conventional recipes, yet the result will be delicious.

For the base:–
3 oz. butter or margarine
2 oz. fine vanilla sugar (page 205)
6 oz. plain flour, 81%
Yolk of 1 egg
Little milk

Cream butter or margarine together until soft and fluffy, beat in egg yolk and finally work in flour. Add a very little milk to make a pliable dough. Knead for a few minutes. Press mixture evenly into bottom of 8-9 inch lined sandwich tin, prick with a fork and bake for 10 minutes at 350°F.

For the filling:–
¾ lb cottage cheese
2 oz. fine vanilla sugar
3 eggs
2 tablespoonsful top of milk or thin cream
½ teaspoonful ground mace or nutmeg

Press cheese through a sieve and beat in sugar. Divide egg yolks from whites, beat yolks, milk or cream into cheese. In a large dry bowl put the 4 egg whites and beat until stiff. Fold into cheese mixture and when thoroughly mixed pour over prepared crust and bake for 1 hour in a moderate 350°F oven. The cake should be a golden brown, so watch it after 45 minutes. Leave for 10 minutes before turning out to cool. Can be chilled in fridge if preferred.

8
VARIETY IN BREAD

This chapter seeks to show that if you bake your own bread you can enjoy a variety of different kinds, sweet and savoury, without much fuss. Baking bread isn't difficult – no more so than baking cakes. It's made to seem difficult because we're 'programmed' to be helpless – that's why people queue, fight each other and go short whenever there's a bread strike. Yet they could be happily baking ten times better bread in their own kitchens in far less time!

When writing about bread we're ever aware of the mighty White versus Wholemeal battle – and by now you'll know which side we back. It's a question of taste and health, and everyone has the right to decide: we can only point out some less well known facts and offer a few opinions. Home-made bread doesn't have to be wholemeal. What counts is whether you can bake at home economically. If you've a range, whether solid fuel or oil-fired, the answer is 'yes' because it will be alight most of the time. If you cook with gas or electricity the answer can be 'yes' if you combine baking with other cooking so that you utilise the oven heat continuously and to the full.

If you buy a wholemeal loaf and suspect it's phoney, send it to your local authority for examination. Wholemeal by law should contain *all* the wheat. Brown bread contains only part of the wheat, though more than white – about 70 per cent extraction – and by law may be coloured with caramel to imitate wholemeal.

For perfect wholemeal bread, baking should begin as soon as the wheat is milled, for once milled, the value of the wheatgerm deteriorates until it eventually goes rancid. So if you invest in your own mill or grinder you can ensure perfection. In time you can recoup the cost of the grinder by buying wheat grains in bulk. Grinding wheat is good exercise too!

Some people, as we have said, are allergic to wheat in any form – as indeed people are to many other foods. If you suspect this, your doctor may be willing to help you identify which foods are the problem. (See books by Dr Richard Mackarness in the Further Reading section). However, allergic reactions are far more likely from eating processed white bread, with its chemical additives, than from eating wholemeal without additives. If wheat should be the problem nevertheless, you may have to switch to rye and barley as alternative cereals. We give recipes using both of them.

Defenders of white bread point out that the beneficial fibre in wholemeal flour also contains a potentially harmful substance, phytic acid, harmful because it reduces the body's ability to absorb the essential mineral, calcium. Their concern has been shown to be unjustified. We now know that the body adapts to the presence of phytic acid. If you are unused to eating wholemeal bread, you simply change over to it gradually. That way you gain all its benefits and take no risks, however slight.

You'll see that in some recipes we mention sieved wholemeal flour. This is one way to 'ease' your family into wholemeal bread. You'll be able to use these sievings instead of oatmeal to make digestive biscuits. For a change of flavour you can add them to muesli and soda bread, and use them for thickening soups and for coating rissoles and so on instead of using breadcrumbs.

One more word about flour: some millers do an 81 per cent extraction, others 85 per cent; either will do in the recipes.

Wholemeal Bread

We make our bread *without kneading* because it saves time and tastes better. It is the way pioneered by Doris Grant over 30 years ago. The first recipe below is the basic one and we follow it with six variations, all using 3 lb of wholemeal flour.

*3 lb 100% wholemeal flour,
stone ground if possible
2 teaspoonsful salt
1 oz. of fresh yeast or
1 pkt of dried yeast
1 heaped teaspoonful honey, sugar
or molasses
About 2 pints warm water*

Put flour into a large warm bowl, add salt and mix well with a strong flat wooden spoon. Measure water by pouring ½ pint boiling water into 1½ pints of cold, ensuring correct temperature. Put yeast and sweetening into a small bowl and mix well. (If using dried yeast make by rules on packet.) Add about ½ pint of the warm water to yeast, mix thoroughly, make a well in centre of flour and pour in yeast mixture. Flick some of flour over yeast and leave until it starts to bubble above flour – about 10 minutes. Starting from centre work in the rest of water a little at a time, bringing flour into centre. Mixture should be slippery, but not too wet. Correct amount of water often depends on the kind of flour and how fine it is ground. Mix very well at this stage, working from outer edge of bowl to centre for about 5 minutes to make sure all flour is taken up. Oil three approx. 8 x 4 inch tins, divide mixture between them, press into shape of tin with well floured hand and set to rise in warm place covered with a floured cloth until dough rises to top of tin. Bake in a preheated 400°F oven for about 45 minutes. If your tins are spread around the oven, about 15 minutes after starting to bake rotate their positions so that they all get the same heat treatment. After baking, your bread will have shrunk from sides of tin. Your loaf will have a flat top. Turn out on to a cooling rack.

Optional Variations:

If you feel like adding some variety to your bread, make one plain loaf, as just described, by taking a third of dough out and putting into one tin, then divide the rest to make the following loaves and rolls.

Herb and Garlic Loaf

Divide the remainder into two. Put one half into a clean oiled warm smaller mixing bowl. Make this into a herb and garlic loaf by adding 1 tablespoonful mixed dried herbs, or two of finely chopped fresh mixed herbs, together with a good sized clove of crushed garlic. Mix these into the dough thoroughly and transfer into second tin, set to rise.

Cheese Loaf

The final portion of dough can be made into a cheese loaf by adding 2 oz., more if liked, grated tasty cheese, mixing in very well. To this you can add some grated onion or chopped chives if liked. Set to rise.

Fruit Loaf

Make this fruit loaf instead of the herb bread. It is so good to serve sometimes instead of cake.

Work into the dough 2 tablespoonsful oil or soft margarine, 3 oz. honey or sugar, 6 oz. sultanas, raisins or mixed fruit. Work thoroughly into dough until all are completely combined. Set to rise in 8 x 4 tin. This will take a little longer to cook than the plain loaf. Let it stand a day before cutting.

Barley or Sprouted Wheat Loaf

Put a teacupful of cooked barley or sprouted wheat (page 234) into a third of the dough. Work in very well with oiled hands. Set to rise and bake about 10 minutes longer than a plain loaf.

Dinner or Lunch Rolls

Generously flour a working surface and knead a portion of the dough for a few minutes with the heel of the hand. Form into a round and roll with both hands into a 'sausage'. Cut up into 12 pieces, form each into a round, place evenly on a floured scone tray set to rise for 20 minutes, bake for about 15 minutes.

Honey Buns

Generously flour a working surface. Put a third of the dough on it and knead for a few minutes. Form into a ball and roll out, turning over constantly and adding more flour if necessary to surface, until you have a piece of dough 12 inches or so square. Spread sparingly with butter or margarine, then honey and roll up into a 'sausage'. Cut into 1½ inch pieces. Spread 2 to 3 tablespoonsful honey into a warmed shallow dish large enough to take the pieces side by side, and place each piece cut side up. Set to rise for 20 minutes. Bake at 350°F middle shelf for 15 to 20 minutes, making sure the honey does not burn. Eat still warm from the oven or keep in tin and warm before eating.

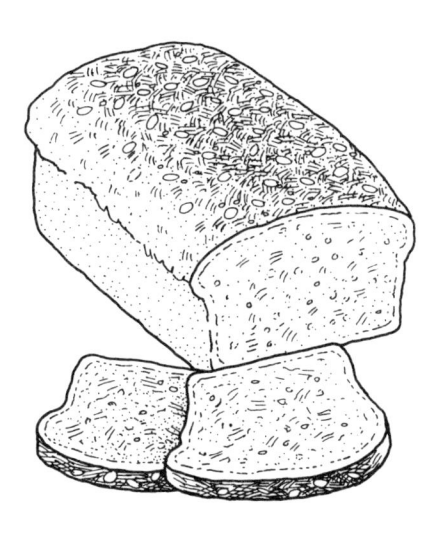

Fancy Bread

A foundation recipe for many fancy breads and buns. Not so rich as conventional ones, but just as good. Here are a few of the possible variations on this theme.

*1 lb sifted wholemeal flour or 81%
or unbleached white
1 egg
2 oz. butter or margarine
2 oz. fine sugar
½ oz. fresh yeast or equivalent
dried yeast
½ teaspoonful salt
About ¼ pint warm milk*

Mix yeast with two teaspoonsful of the sugar and some of the warm milk. Leave to bubble about 10 minutes. Melt butter or margarine in rest of milk. Put flour, salt, rest of sugar in a warm bowl and mix well. Beat egg until frothy. Make a well in centre of flour, add yeast, egg, butter and warm milk mixture, and with a wooden spoon work flour into it from the sides, making a fairly thick batter. Work together for a few minutes until all ingredients are thoroughly combined. Set in a warm place covered, for about 1 hour until doubled in size. When ready oil a hand and knead lightly. Transfer to a floured board and divide into two. Knead lightly each piece. Leave one half in bowl and cover to keep warm. Make one piece into a tea ring.

Tea Ring

Roll out, turning often, on the well floured surface, into a square about ¼ inch or less thick, spread lightly with butter or margarine and scatter over about 2 oz. of mixed dried fruit and some freshly grated nutmeg. Moisten all edges, roll up like a Swiss roll. Push ends into each other to form a ring. To keep its shape, transfer to a well oiled pie dish, push towards the edge leaving centre clear and snip the ring at 1½ inch intervals with scissors. Set to raise for about 20 minutes. Bake at 400°F for 20 to 30 minutes on lower shelf until golden. While still hot, glaze with honey or thin icing and decorate with nuts, angelica and so on. Serve warm.

Breakfast Rolls (Brioches)
Knead lightly the other half of the dough again, and with the palm of the hands roll into a sausage shape. Cut into 12 even portions. Oil brioche moulds or patty tins. Make each portion into a neat ball and set in the tins and allow to raise for 20 to 30 minutes. Bake at 400°F for 10 to 15 minutes. Glaze with honey or sugared water immediately.

Apple Slice
Roll out half the quantity of dough as for tea ring and lightly butter. Slice enough sweet apples very thinly to cover half the rolled dough. Sprinkle with demarara sugar and cinnamon to your liking. Dampen edges and fold over. Place on a scone tray and cut slits into the dough to let out the steam and make attractive. Bake at 300°F for about 30 minutes and glaze with honey or thin icing.
Use the same recipe for hot cross buns and Bath buns.

Hot Cross Buns
Add to flour in foundation mixture 2 teaspoonful or 1 oz. of mixed spice. Soak 4 oz. currants or sultanas in a little warm water to plump them up, drain and dry well. Before setting to rise fold in the sultanas until all are evenly distributed. After rising, shape into about 18 buns and roll flat. Place on scone trays to rise again for about 15 minutes. Just before you put them in oven cut a cross with a sharp knife. Bake for about 20 minutes. As you take them out, glaze with sugar water or melted butter.

Bath Buns

Using the basic recipe, add 2 oz. soaked sultanas and some candied peel to the mixture before setting to rise. Divide into 18 pieces, form into rounds. Roll once. Place on a greased and floured baking tray. Cover each one with a little sugar water and a generous sprinkling with demarara sugar lightly pressed into dough. Set to rise for 15 minutes in a warm place. Bake at 400°F middle shelf for 20 minutes.

Continental Coffee Cake

Borrowed from Germany, this is not a coffee-flavoured cake but one which, although traditionally eaten with coffee, can be enjoyed at any time without the coffee. The important part of this cake is the topping which imparts a deceptive richness.

Use half the quantity of the dough in foundation recipe. After it has risen, press into a well oiled 7 x 7 x 2 inch tin (about). Make a topping by mixing together 2 oz. sugar, 2 oz. butter or margarine, 2 oz. flour, a flat tablespoonful of ground almonds or a few drops essence, 1 teaspoonful cinnamon with just enough milk to make a smooth paste. Spread over the top of the dough, put into the oven immediately and bake for about 20 to 30 minutes at 350°F. Serve warm.

Regulations define wholemeal bread as being composed of dough made from wholemeal, yeast and water, without the addition of any other flour. Wholemeal is required to contain the whole of the product derived from the milling of clean wheat. Any member of the public who suspects that a loaf labelled 'wholemeal' has not been made from wholemeal is at liberty to purchase the loaf, and send it to the local authority for examination.

Malt Loaf

The barley in this low-sugar recipe imparts a pleasantly different texture.

¾ lb wholemeal flour
1 teacupful cooked pearl barley
2 oz. honey or sugar
2 tablespoonsful molasses
2 tablespoonsful malt extract
4 oz. sultanas, raisins or mixed fruit if liked
¼ pint milk or more
1 teaspoonful bicarbonate of soda
¼ teaspoonful salt
Grated nutmeg if liked

In large bowl combine thoroughly flour, salt and spice if used. Add dried fruit. Put milk, molasses, honey (or sugar) and malt extract into a pan and warm over low flame to just under blood heat, stirring to combine. Make a well in flour and pour in milk mixture. Add barley and soda, combine thoroughly, bringing flour to centre until all is very well mixed and barley completely dispersed. The mixture should be slightly wet, so add more milk if necessary. Pour into a lined 8 x 4 inch approx. bread tin and bake in a moderate oven 350° to 375°F for 1 hour or until a knife inserted comes out clean. Cool in tin and leave for a day before cutting. Eat with butter or cream cheese.

'Desperation' Bread or Soda Round

Suppose you run out of bread, you've neither wholemeal flour nor yeast in the house, and only an hour before lunch for hearty appetites! No need to make a panic dash to the shops. Either of these two ways of making quick, wholesome bread will solve your problem. And, just supposing you had a power cut as well, you'll bless the knowledge that one of the ways needs nothing more than a fry pan and a gas ring or camping stove!

10 oz. white flour
2 oz. porridge oats
2 oz. sievings from wholemeal flour
or 1 oz. bran
½ pint or more of sour milk
though fresh will do
1 tablespoonful baking powder
or 2 teaspoonsful cream tartar and
1 teaspoonful bicarb soda
¼ teaspoonful salt

Put porridge oats and sievings or bran in a large bowl. Pour over sour milk and soak for 20 minutes in a warm place. If you have less time, use hot fresh milk and soak for 10 minutes. Mix thoroughly together flour, salt and baking powder and fold into mixture. It should be like a rather damp scone mixture, so add a little more milk if necessary. If you use soda and cream tartar, beat them into milk mixture before adding flour. Divide into two well-oiled sandwich tins or an 8 x 2 inch tin and bake in pre-heated oven at 400°F for about 30 to 45 minutes on middle shelf. If using two tins the time will be shorter.

For the fry pan method, put a heavy-based pan on a medium heat and when quite hot sprinkle with flour. Press mixture over base and flour top. If you don't have a lid turn a tin plate upside down over the top. Cook for 15 to 20 minutes, then turn over and cook the other side for another 10 minutes until a golden brown. For this method you can divide the mixture into small rounds and make into girdle scones instead.

Brown Scones

Quick and easy to make, these scones are another way to put right a breadless predicament. Extra tempting served hot, and even more so with any one of the variations.

½ lb sifted wholemeal flour
(or half wholemeal, half white)
1 egg
1 oz. fat or 1 tablespoonful oil
3 teaspoonsful baking powder
¼ teaspoonful salt
Some warm milk

Mix dry ingredients thoroughly. Beat up egg, mix fat or oil into flour, make a well and pour in egg and some milk. Mix very well, adding extra milk until you have made a soft dough. Knead for a minute on a floured board, roll or pat out to about ½ inch thick, cut into rounds and place on warmed tray and bake briskly at 400°F for 10 to 15 minutes.

Optional variations:
Add 2 teaspoonsful sugar or 2 oz. mixed fruit or 2 teaspoonsful caraway seeds or 1 teaspoonful mixed spice. For a savoury scone add 1 or 2 oz. grated tasty cheese and 1 tablespoonful chopped gherkin.

Rye Bread

Rye with its sharper flavour can make a welcome change from wheat. It may suit those with an allergy to wheat too.

2½ lb rye flour
1 oz. yeast
1 tablespoonful honey or sugar
1 tablespoonful oil
1½ pints warm water
1 teaspoonful salt
1 tablespoonful caraway seed (optional)

Cream the yeast with honey and some of the water, add rest of water and oil to the flour and salt in a warm bowl. Mix thoroughly. Cover very well and leave overnight in a warm place. Divide dough into two or more and shape into oval loaves. Set to rise on a floured baking sheet until double in size. Bake in moderate 350°F oven for 1 to 1½ hours.

When making scones or bread don't give the dough a shock by using cold tins or trays, but always have them really warm. Oil is the best to use for bread tins. Never wash them. When the bread is cooked properly it should slide out of the tins cleanly so there is no need ever to wash them.

Breads can be cooked in earthenware plant pots, only they must be floured not greased. Cooked this way the bread is really crusty. Try it!

Welsh Barley Bread

Barley was once the grain for all bread of 'the ordinary folk', You'll find it heavier that wheat or rye ... you may even prefer it for a change. Try it anyway. Another kind of bread for anyone allergic to wheat.

4 teacupsful barley flour
2 teaspoonsful honey or sugar
1 teacupful warm water
1 oz. yeast
1 teaspoonful salt

Mix yeast with honey and a little of warm water. Set aside to froth then, with wooden spoon, fold into the flour and salt with the rest of the water and mix until well blended. Set dough to rise for an hour. Knead lightly and place in a well oiled 8 inch sandwich tin. Bake at 400°F for 25 to 30 minutes or until loaf sounds hollow when tapped on underside.

9
THIS AND THAT

In this chapter you will find some recipes for stocks and 'accessories' which you can use with recipes appearing in more than one of the preceding chapters. There are also some preserves and useful recipes which don't rightly belong in any other chapter.

In the last category we include home-made beverages, for many of which we give detailed recipes. We haven't done so for home-made wines and cider, and for home-brewed beer. We hasten to add that this isn't because we frown on the practice. We changed from buying commercial wines, spirits and beers some time ago in favour of making our own wine. We enjoy what we make. Unlike commercial liquor it's additive-free. Apart from the yeast and sugar, the ingredients are homegrown. And it's almost unbelievably cheaper – we developed a deep resentment to paying in tax far more than the cost of the ingredients in every bottle. The reason why we haven't included recipes is that to do so would really have meant writing another book. There are dozens to choose from already.

Boiled Wheat

Many people would never think of cooking whole wheat grains (or berries), yet they resemble brown rice and are often thought to better them in flavour. Use in sweet or savoury dishes.

Soak a teacupful of wheat grains overnight in cold water. Pour into sieve and rinse. Put in pan with 2½ teacupsful of water. Simmer slowly until tender – about 1 hour, or use a pressure cooker as directed. Never use salted water but add seasoning later.

Bulgur Wheat

This ancient recipe is almost as old as the first farmers. Simmering, then light roasting the wheat grains, imparts a nutty flavour to them. Bulgur can be added to bread, stuffings and salads, or eaten at breakfast in porridge or on its own as a cereal. Whichever way you eat it, no more cooking is needed – merely soaking. Wholefood shops sell it, but you will save by making it yourself this easy way: our recipe is for a trial amount while you decide whether you agree with the ancients.

1 teacupful wheat
2½ teacupsful boiling water

Put the wheat in a sieve and shake to remove any powder, then wash under running cold tap for a few seconds, moving it about. Put in a strong pan, pour boiling water over and simmer gently for about 45 minutes or until it has absorbed all the water and doubled in size. Spread out on a scone tray or flat tins and dry in a 200°F oven. While drying move it around occasionally. When completely dry and crisp and lightly browned, cool then store in an airtight jar.

Bulgur in Bread
For a change of texture when baking wholemeal bread, add 1 tablespoonful to a 1 lb loaf. Just soak in hot water for 30 minutes, drain through a sieve, and, to remove excess water, squeeze it. Work into the dough before setting to rise in tin.

Bulgur in Salad
Soak bulgur in hot water and when cold drain and add to a grated root vegetable salad for extra flavour and nourishment.

Bulgur for Breakfast
Soak some bulgur overnight, by pouring over hot milk or water, and add it to porridge; or enjoy it with milk or yogurt and dried fruit, sliced apple or anything else you fancy.

Bulgur and Meat

These ingredients will help to make meat go further.

Chopped or minced cooked meat
2 teacupsful bulgur
4 teacupsful stock
1 large onion
Diced carrot
Some celery
Any other vegetables you fancy
Some herbs, coriander
Little oil or butter
Salt and pepper

Put oil or butter in a large pan and sauté vegetables for a few minutes. Add bulgur, stock, herbs and seasoning, and simmer for about 15 minutes. Stir in cooked meat and serve as soon as meat is heated through. You can use this recipe as stuffing for a marrow.

No Fuss Sprouted Wheat

We find this the easiest way to sprout wheat for winter vitamin C, and to add to salads or eat with yogurt as a breakfast cereal – or any other way you choose.

1 teacupful wheat berries
Some water

Wash berries in plenty of water, put in a sieve and hold under running tap. Place in an earthenware dish. Cover with cold water and put a lid or plate on top. After 12 hours pour this water off into a bowl and use as stock for soups. Wash thoroughly again, cover with water and stand for 12 hours more. Wash and put back in dish without water. Keep covered for 24 hours. Wash again and proceed in this way for 2 more days, by which time the wheat will be nicely sprouted. Keep in fridge or cool place and use before the sprouts grow too long.

Muesli

If you're looking for foods where you part with the most money in exchange for the least nutrients, you needn't look much further than the average breakfast cereal. Don't be fooled by their impressive lists of added vitamins and so on. These over-advertised, over-packaged processed foods are the most expensive way of eating plain grains man ever devised. Instead try making your own. Here's an economical basic muesli recipe to start with. You can add to it or vary the proportions to suit the family's taste.

4 oz. flaked oats
2 oz. flaked barley
3 oz. mixed chopped nuts
2 oz. ground almonds
3 oz. raisins

Simply shake all together in a jar and keep airtight. To add interest to this basic recipe add a sprinkling of wheat, boiled or sprouted, or soaked bulgur wheat. Remember muesli is delicious served with yogurt instead of milk.

For less than what the world spends on armies and armaments in a single year, world hunger could be eliminated. For if poverty were banished, population growth would slow down, and improved, appropriate farming methods could match supply with demand.

Vegetable Stock

When preparing root vegetables, always scrub clean first and if they are very fresh from the garden do not peel, just cut out any uneatable pieces. If skins are tough, peel as thinly as possible and use for the stock pot. As well as all the root vegetables the following can be used if cleaned very well. Potato peelings, outer stalks and tops of celery (inner tops go into salad), outsides and dark green parts of leeks, outer leaves of all green vegetables, the tough inner skins of onions. Only use potato peelings if you want a mild stock for a delicate dish. To make your stock, cover the vegetables with water and either pressure cook for 30 minutes or simmer gently on top of stove for about 1 hour. Strain first through a colander into a bowl, then press the vegetables down with weighted saucer and leave over a dish for an hour or so. It is surprising how much moisture the cooked vegetables will release. Refrigerate according to the star rating. Try to use within three days.

Chicken Stock

Make this from the bones and skin of cooked chicken. Pull carcase apart and cover with hot water to about an inch above the bones. Simmer about 1½ hours in a strong pan or 30 minutes in pressure cooker. Strain through a sieve, and allow to get cold. The ensuing thick jelly will have some fat on top which needs to be carefully skimmed off. Keep jelly in fridge according to star rating. Put the fat in a strong pan and boil for a few minutes until the rest of the moisture has evaporated. Useful for Chinese cooking or for other poultry recipes.

'Hot' Cucumber Chutney

With this spicey recipe, summer's abundance will enliven winter dishes.

4 lb cucumber, weighed after seeding
2 lb green tomatoes
6 fresh red chillies, seeds and all
(More if you like it even hotter!)
1½ lb sugar
1 pint vinegar
1½ teaspoonsful freshly ground allspice
1 teaspoonful freshly ground cloves
2 large cloves garlic
Plenty of salt

Select a large bowl. Cut cucumber lengthwise and remove centres with silver spoon. Peel if necessary. Cut again lengthwise and then into pieces. Weigh 1 lb prepared cucumber, place in bowl and cover generously with salt. Repeat in layers, 1 lb at a time, remembering to finish with salt covering. Leave covered to stand for 24 hours. Then wash cucumber in colander under running water to remove salt. Dry with cloth. Put in preserving pan with tomatoes (cut up but not too small), chillies (cut into fine rings, wearing rubber gloves if you have sensitive skin), sugar, vinegar, spices and 2 teaspoonsful salt. Cook over gentle heat until sugar has dissolved, then over higher heat, 1 to 1½ hours until thick – making sure it doesn't burn. Transfer to hot, clean jars as for jam. Cover when cold. Makes about 4 lb.

Saté Sauce

Pronounced 'sartay', this Javanese 'hot' sauce is easy to make and will add a tingling spiciness to a variety of dishes – root vegetables or grains especially – for winter or summer eating. Try adding a dash to mayonnaise to enliven a potato salad.

2 oz. dried mustard
3 teaspoonsful cayenne pepper
¼ pint cider vinegar
2 tablespoonsful honey

Mix mustard and pepper thoroughly in a bowl, add vinegar and work to a paste, then mix in honey. Put in a screw-top jar and shake well before using sparingly.

Tomato Sauce

Save buying expensive tomato purée and make your own with tomatoes from shop – or, better still, from your own garden when they are plentiful and cheapest. It's easy to make, but because it contains no preservative, don't keep it longer than a couple of days in the fridge before use.

2 lb ripe tomatoes
1 medium chopped onion
1 clove garlic
1 teaspoonful sweet basil
1 teaspoonful sugar
Salt and pepper

Cook all ingredients gently for 30 minutes with pan lid on to reduce to a pulp. Put all through a sieve. Cook again if you want it thicker. Use it for any dish which requires a strong tomato flavour.

Tomato Ketchup

Make this appetising sauce when tomatoes are abundant in the garden and cheap in the shops. A good way to make use of imperfect ones. If stored in a cool place, it should keep for six months.

6 lb ripe tomatoes
1½ lb onions
1½ lb sugar
1½ pints vinegar
¼ teaspoonful cayenne pepper
½ oz. freshly ground peppercorns
1 oz. freshly ground allspice
15 whole cloves
2 oz. salt

Wipe tomatoes and cut up roughly with stainless steel knife on a plate. Peel and cut up onions very fine. Put tomatoes and onions in a preserving pan and gently bring to the boil. Add sugar, vinegar and salt. When sugar has melted, start to cook quickly and keep stirring to make sure the mixture doesn't stick. Now add the spices. Boil gently for one hour, then sieve into large bowl. Return to preserving pan and boil for a further 10 minutes. Have ready 3 pint bottles or 6 half pint bottles, washed and heating in a 300°F oven. Sterilize a kitchen funnel by boiling in water for 5 minutes. Take bottles out of oven one at a time and, as you remove each one, fill with boiling ketchup to 1 inch from top. Cork immediately.

Of the 17 million tonnes of grain Britain grows each year, about two-thirds is eaten by farm livestock – three million tonnes by pigs alone.

Green Tomato Mincemeat

Also a delicious pie filling, this preserve retains no taste of the green tomatoes which form its base. Not too sweet, it is low in sugar, but on account of this, use it within two months of making.

4 lb green tomatoes
2 lb eating apples
1 lb raisins or sultanas
¼ pint cider vinegar
¼ pint molasses
½ lb sugar
1 orange
1 lemon – optional
2 teaspoonsful ground cinnamon
4 cloves

Wash and wipe tomatoes, cut into four, then into chunks and put in preserving pan. Wipe apples, cut into 4, core then chop roughly and add to pan. Add raisins, vinegar, molasses, sugar and spices. If using orange and lemon, wash well, cut into 4, take out any pips, cut up very fine, or mince, then add to pan. Heat slowly at first to melt sugar and then boil quickly for 30 minutes. Put in hot jars and cover in usual way.
You will find it fairly runny, so when you make a pie with it sprinkle some corn flour over the fruit before adding the top crust. This will absorb excess liquid.

Green Tomato Jam

This excellent way of using up green tomatoes – abundant about every other year – will keep most people guessing, for it tastes and looks remarkably like fresh fig jam. Always a favourite in our house.

4 lb tomatoes
3 lb sugar
2 teaspoonsful ground ginger or
grated rind of a lemon or both

Cut tomatoes roughly. Put in preserving pan over a very low heat. Cook them until juice starts to run and bring to the boil, then remove from heat. Stir in sugar 1 lb at a time until all completely melted. Add ginger and or lemon at this stage, bring back to boiling and boil for 20-30 minutes. Pot in hot jars and cover in usual way.

Spiced Apple

This is an easy and delicious way of storing an embarrassment of apples – a stiff, amber preserve for cakes (see page 209), tarts and puddings. You can either make plenty at a time or, with the quantities listed, just enough to keep pace with bruised windfalls. The preserve will keep for a long time without the bother of sterilizing and bottling or the disquietingly high sugar content of jam.

4 lb apples (after peeling, coring and removing bruises)
2 lb sugar
¼ pint vinegar
¼ pint water
Cloves or any other spice you fancy

Place all in a bowl and leave overnight. Transfer to a preserving pan and bring slowly to boil. Boil for an hour or more until dark amber. Transfer to hot jars and cover when cool.

When making jam or jelly, use only ¾ lb sugar to each 1 lb of fruit.

Fluffy Dumplings

Mention dumplings and most people think of stodgy lumps of suet, flour and water. Ugh! Dumplings should always be light and fluffy, and they can either be plain or laced with herbs, cheese or meat. You'll be amply repaid for the little extra trouble that this recipe entails.

¼ lb sifted wholemeal flour
½ teaspoonful baking powder
Good pinch salt
1½ oz. butter or margarine
1 egg

Mix flour, baking powder and salt in bowl. Work in fat until consistency of breadcrumbs. Whisk egg. Make a well in flour mixture, pour in egg and mix well but lightly. Mixture should be soft but not too wet. If too dry add a little water. Divide into 4, roll in flour and add to casseroles or stews to simmer for 15 minutes before serving.

Optional variations:
Half white/half wholemeal flour
1 tablespoonful finely chopped parsley
2 teaspoonsful mixed herbs
Some tasty cheese
Cooked ham
Onions

Use your imagination to create variations. You can reduce the fat to 1 oz. and add 1 oz. grated tasty cheese or pieces of cooked ham. Or you can simply add parsley and mixed herbs. Or, if you fancy onion, add 2 teaspoonsful grated and reduce the amount of egg if mixture looks like being too wet.

Yogurt

It's not surprising that this ancient way of using and preserving milk – from cow and goat – has become a minor cult. It tastes good and it's good for you. But that's not the end of the story! Its modern ingredients are but a tiny fraction of the price you pay, for they're mostly left-overs from cheese and butter-making and the E.E.C. dairy product 'mountains'. The principal costs you incur when you buy your pretty carton are transport, processing, packaging and profit. What's more, nearly all makes contain sugar – a major factor in the cult's popularity – as well as other dubious additives. So, if you do buy, read the small print!

Most people know you can make your own. What they may not realise is just how easy it is to do so, how much money you save when you do, and what an infinitely superior and purer product you create. For the *real* thing is milk in a more digestible form which also aids the digestion of other food and synthesizes vitamin B.

No need to buy a pricey electric yogurt-maker. Use a wide-necked Thermos, a picnic food container, or simply a glass jar in a hay box or one filled with left-over insulating material such as polystyrene beads. They all work well.

There are plenty of methods to choose from, but whichever you use, you'll need a starter. This can be a little plain yogurt from a friend, or a laboratory culture. Use a starter made from cow's milk for cow's milk yogurt, or one from goat's milk for goat's milk yogurt. Otherwise they may not work properly. (For culture suppliers see Ideas for Action section).

Here's one recipe we were given by a friend. Scald 2 pints of milk and cool to blood heat, then add 2 tablespoonsful of yogurt. In your container keep it at the required temperature – 70 to 100°F – for at least 4 hours. Then cool. Save 2 tablespoonsful for the next batch.

If you prefer it thick, add 4 tablespoonsful of dried milk to the 2 pints when blood heat and beat in well. If you're not used to natural yogurt, add honey or fresh fruit, cut up.

Instead of Tea and Coffee ...

As we have recommended, to follow The Small Island Diet means to drink less tea and coffee. Now this isn't at all easy – as we can personally testify! Fortunately you can make your own hot and cold beverages to take their place – if not all the time, at least often enough to make a really significant difference to your tea and coffee intake. With the possible exception of dandelion coffee – which we find infinitely preferable to 'railway' and other varieties of the real tortured thing – none of these beverages is a true *substitute*, indeed to look on them as such is to anticipate disappointment. Instead, if trying them for the first time, think of each one as a new experience and judge it on its own merit, not as some imitation of a familiar drink. You will soon select what you like and maybe dislike.

Remember though that each and every one has at least two big advantages over 'the hard stuff': they are good for you, as opposed to harmful in excess; and they can be absolutely free. And if you want one more advantage as well – no growers or pickers are being exploited in the Poor South.

Let's look at recipes for 'coffee type' drinks first.

Dandelion

Dig dandelion roots in March and April before the plant begins to flower, or in September and October before they rest for the winter. Cut off tops. Scrub off soil in plenty of water and dry well. Cut into thin strips where necessary, lay on a baking sheet and cook slowly in a 300°F oven until browned through. They must be crisp but not burned. Store in an airtight jar.
Grind as required.

Just one teaspoonful for each person's cup is enough. Put required number of spoonfuls in a pan, pour over the right amount of hot water, bring slowly to the boil, pop lid on and infuse for four minutes. Strain off, re-heat if necessary and serve black or with hot milk.

You shouldn't need sugar for this drink – or *any* of the home-made beverages, so that is another plus point for them!

Parsnip

Scrub roots clean and take off any bad parts. Grate coarsely and sprinkle on a baking sheet. Roast in a fairly hot oven at 400°F for 15 to 20 minutes. Watch them carefully for they must be dark brown – not cinders. No need to grind them. Store in an airtight jar. Use a dessertspoonful for each cup and make the same as dandelion except infuse for five minutes, not four.

Grain

Use barley, wheat or rye – or a blend of two or three of these grains. Simply roast in a 350° oven until dark brown, turning occasionally. Again, watch they don't burn. Store in an airtight jar. Grind as required. Use a teaspoonful or more for each cup, according to preference. Make as for parsnip. This is a subtler, milder beverage than the other two.

Any of these beverages may be mixed with coffee itself if you want to make it go further. You could try gradually reducing the proportion of coffee as a way to cut down.

Herb Teas

As the price of tea soars and the quality of blends deteriorates, the case for effective counter-action becomes stronger. Tea is a drug, and the merchants know that it will sell, even though they add increasing proportions of poorer teas, simply because users have become 'hooked'. If you don't believe that quality has suffered, splash out on a top grade Ceylon or Indian tea just for once and compare.

Perhaps the best action is to embark on breaking the tea habit, saving the drink for special occasions when you can enjoy the finest tea, and drinking your own herb teas in between. You may get to like them so much that, after a little perseverance, 'kicking' the tea habit turns out to be less of a problem than you expect. If you simply can't break it, try reducing the number of times a day you have a cuppa, and stick to one rather than have two or three. One tip worth noting is this: you can make your own Earl Grey mixture at no extra cost compared with ordinary tea by adding your own, home-grown Bergamot leaves – after drying – to a good Indian blend.

There are too many different kinds of herb teas for us to list in full. Plenty of books on the subject have been written, and we suggest *Food for Free* (see Further Reading section). Ones that we enjoy include the leaves of blackberry and raspberry bushes; flowers of camomile, clover and elderberry; and leaves of the herbs sage, hyssopp, lemon balm and mint – especially peppermint. All these can be made into 'tea' fresh or dried. Drying is simple. We snip a few holes in the bottom of a large paper bag, pile the flowers or leaves in loosely, tie the top and hang over the stove. We look at them once a week, and, when really crisp, pack them into airtight tins or dark jars –ones used for malt extract are ideal. The paper bags, by the way, keep flies off. An alternative method is to hang or lay the paper bags in an airing cupboard.

Tea made from flowers is even better if their first drying is in the sun. We pick as soon as the dew is off the blooms, lay them on a flat tray in the sun, cover with muslin to keep the flies off, and bring indoors well before the evening dew. Of all the 'teas' blackberry leaves can make you the one closest to the real thing – if that is your wish. The secret is to ferment them a while in water before drying. To make your 'tea', brew in the normal way, though usually for rather longer.

Vary the amounts to suit your taste.

Whatever you make can afford you more satisfaction than handing over money for fancy packages and dainty bags, offered at fancy prices.

You can buy a high grade Ceylon tea and also good instant coffee through Traidcraft, an organization campaigning for justice for Poor South producers. Competitively priced, the beverages still benefit producers more than do well-known brands marketed by multi-national companies. For details send SAE to Traidcraft, India House, Carliol Square, Newcastle-upon-Tyne NE1 6TY.

Ideas For Action

When writing to any of these organisations, remember to send stamps or S.A.E. and please mention this book.

Growing Your Own Food
For advice and regular publication of information on growing food organically, without poisons and chemicals, join the Henry Doubleday Research Association, 20 Convent Lane, Bocking, Braintree, Essex; or the Soil Association, Walnut Tree Manor, Haughley, Stowmarket, Suffolk, IP14 3RS., or both.

Subscribe to *Practical Self-Sufficiency*, bi-monthly magazine, Broad Leys Publishing Co., Widdington, Essex, CB11 35P.

Experience of Country Life
Support 'City Farms' – projects involving animals and gardening on otherwise wasted city plots, especially popular with young people. Write City Farms, Inter-Action Trust Ltd., 15 Wilkin Street, London, NW5.

Join WWOOF (Working Weekends on Organic Farms), Main Office: 19 Bradford Road, Lewes, Sussex, BN7 1RB. Work, tuition and good company in exchange for board and keep.

Preserving Fruit and Vegetables
Get information on all aspects from Long Ashton Research Station, University of Bristol, Long Ashton, Bristol, BS18 9AF.

Natural and Wholefood Supplies
Take a step to free yourself from chemical additives and order from people such as:–
Organically grown wheat and flour and other cereals:
S. Mayall & Son, Lea Hall, Harmer Hill, Shrewsbury, SY4 3DY.
Yogurt culture:
Christian Hansen's Laboratories Ltd., Mansfield House, 376 Strand, London WC2, and Fullwood and Bland Ltd., Ellesmere, Shropshire.
Natural essences and herbs:
Culpepper Ltd., 21 Bruton Street, London, W1X 7DA, and local branches.

Nutrition and Health
Join the McCarrison Society, founded to study the relationship between the two, and placing emphasis on disease prevention through fresh, whole food and balanced diet. Write The Treasurer, the McCarrison Society, Forest Field, Leicester Lane, Desford, Leics.

Factory Farming
Learn more about how most veal, pork, bacon and eggs are produced, and help to end cruelty. Write to Compassion in World Farming, Lyndum House, Petersfield, Hampshire, GU32 3JG.

World Poverty and Hunger
Learn more about development and join or form local branches. Write World Development Movement, Bedford Chambers, Covent Garden, London, WC2E 8HA.

Subscribe to *New Internationalist*, monthly magazine focussing attention on the unjust relationship between rich and poor worlds, debating and campaigning for necessary radical change. Montague House, High Street, Huntingdon, Cambridgeshire, PE18 6EP.

Support Oxfam, 274 Banbury Road, Oxford, OX2 7DZ. and War on Want, 467 Caledonian Road, London, N7.

Further Reading

Growing food:
Complete Self-Sufficiency, John Seymour (Faber 1976).
The Complete Urban Farmer, David Wickers (Friedmann 1976).
Grow Your Own Fruit and Vegetables, Lawrence Hills (Faber 1971).
Herb Gardening, Clair Loewenfeld (Faber 1970).
Living on a Little Land, Patrick Rivers (Turnstone 1978).

Nutrition and health:
Chemical Victims, Dr Richard Mackarness (Pan 1980).
Diet For a Small Planet, Frances Moore Lappé (Ballantine U.S.).
Eating For Health, Department of Health (HMSO 1978).
Manual of Nutrition, Ministry of Agriculture (HMSO 1976).
Not All in the Mind, Dr Richard Mackarness (Pan 1976).
Pure White and Deadly, John Yudkin (Davis Poynter 1972).
This Nutrition Business, John Yudkin (David Poynter 1976).

Cooking:
Future Cook, Colin Tudge (Mitchell Beazley 1980).
The Garden Grows Cookbook, Eva Lambert and Tony Lambert (Wildwood 1978).
The Subversive Vegetarian, Michael Cox and Desda Crockett (Thorsons, 1979).

Food and agriculture policies:
An Agricultural Strategy for the UK, (Centre for Agricultural Strategy 1977).
Can Britain Feed Itself?, Kenneth Mellanby (Merlin 1975).
Farming and the Nation, (HMSO 1979).
National Food Policy in the UK, (Centre for Agricultural Strategy 1979).

Rich North and Poor South:
Food First, Frances Moore Lappé and Joseph Collins (Souvenir 1980).
Inside the Third World, Paul Harrison (Penguin 1979).
New Internationalist Magazine, especially Nos. 42 & 43 on 'Meeting Basic Needs'.

General:
Food for Free, Richard Mabey (Fontana 1976).
Food in History, Reay Tannahill (Paladin 1975).
Living Better on Less, Patrick Rivers (Turnstone 1977).

RECIPE INDEX

Apple Slice, 223
Artichoke Soup, 78

Baked Barley, 147
Baked Fruity Batter, 207
Baked Shaggy Caps, 118
Baked Smoked Mackerel, 172
Baked Stuffed Cucumbers, 130
Barley or Sprouted Wheat
  Loaf, 220
Barley Vegetable Soup, 79
Basic White Sauce, 190
Bath Buns, 224
Bean Spread, 145
Bean Rissoles, 144
Bean Roast, 134
Beef and Ham Roll, 157
Blackcurrant Ice, 199
Boiled Fowl with Bacon and
  Herbs, 158
Boiled Wheat, 232
Braised Red Cabbage, 113
Breakfast Rolls, 223
Brioches, *see* Breakfast Rolls
Brown Scones, 227
Brussels Sprouts and Celeriac
  Salad, 99
Bulgur and Meat, 233
Bulgur for Breakfast, 233
Bulgur in Bread, 233
Bulgur in Salad, 233
Bulgur Wheat, 232
Bulgur Wheat Salad, 104

Carrot and Potato Pancakes,
  125
Carrot, Apple and Sprouted
  Wheat Salad, 98
Casserole of Mackerel or
  Herring, 173
Casserole of Pigeons with
  Red Wine, 164

Casserole of Rabbit, 166
Celeriac Croquettes, 126
Celeriac Soup, 80
Cheese Cake, 216
Cheese Flan, 154
Cheese Loaf, 220
Chestnut Soup, 81
Chestnut Stuffing, 189
Chicken and Vegetable with
  Noodles, 176
Chicken Mayonnaise, 161
Chicken Stock, 236
Chilled Cucumber Soup, 84
Chinese Noodles, 175
Continental Coffee Cake, 224
Cooked Mayonnaise, 106
Cornish Pasties, 162
Cottage Cheese and Honey
  Flan, 203
Croûtons for Soup and Salads,
  93
Crunchy Sprouts and Broccoli,
  111
Cucumber Raita, 100

Dandelion Coffee, 245
'Desperation' Bread, 226
Dhal, 181
Dinner or Lunch Rolls, 221
Dried Haricot Bean Salad, 99

Eggless Spice Cake, 214
English Salad, 100

Fancy Bread, 222
Fish Salad, 101
Flan Pastry, 202
Fluffy Dumplings, 243
Forcemeat, 188
Fruit Crumble, 210
Fruit Delight, 197
Fruit Loaf, 220

Frumenty, 212

Galantine of Chicken, 160
Garlic Dressing, 107
Gazpacho, 82
Grain Coffee, 246
Green Tomato Jam, 241
Green Tomato Mincemeat, 240

Herb and Garlic Loaf, 220
Herb Teas, 246-7
Home-made Pasta, 186
Honey Buns, 221
Hot Cross Buns, 223
'Hot' Cucumber Chutney, 237
Hot Sweet Corn, 128

Jerusalem Artichokes, 114
Jerusalem Artichokes with Sprouts, 115

Leek and Potato Pie, 131
Leek Soup, 85
Lettuce Soup, 86

Malt Loaf, 225
Meat Balls, 169
Meat Curry, 182
Medieval Parsnip Pie, 206
Mixed Fruit Dessert, 198
Mixed Green Garden Salad, 95
Muesli, 235

Nettle Soup, 87
No Fuss Sprouted Wheat, 234

Parsley Soup, 88
Parsnip Coffee, 246
Pasta Sauce, 191
Pears in Elderberry Wine, 198
Pickled Cucumber Salad, 98
Pizza Pie, 184
Plain Sponge Cake, 213
Plum Layer Pudding, 208

Plum Surprise, 201
Pork and Hot Sweet Corn, 129
Potato and Tomato Casserole, 112
Potato Cheese Casserole with Cider, 138
Potato Gnocchi, 187
Potato Salad, 102
Puffball Soup, 89
Pumpkin Soup, 90
Pumpkin Surprise, 117

Quick Mayonnaise, 105
Quick Oil and Vinegar Dressing, 108
Quick Sponge Topping, 211

Raw Beetroot Salad, 96
Real Custard, 204
Roast Rabbit, 165
Roast Stuffed Shoulder of Mutton or Lamb, 163
Rye Bread, 228

Saté Sauce, 238
Sauce for Summer Vegetables, 121
Savoury Batter, 150
Savoury Cauliflower, 124
Savoury Pancake Layers, 152
Savoury Poached Eggs, 148
Savoury Sliced Pumpkin, 116
Shepherd's Pie, 170
Soda Round, see 'Desperation' Bread
Special Cooked Apple, 196
Spiced Apple, 242
Spiced Apple Cake, 209
Spinach Bake, 140
Sponge Cake without Fat, 215
Stewed Plums, 195
Stewed Rhubarb, 195
Stuffed Aubergines, 122
Stuffed Baked Potatoes, 137

RECIPE INDEX

Stuffed Cabbage, 123
Stuffed Eggs in Wine Sauce, 149
Stuffed Green Peppers, 136
Stuffed Marrow, 132
Stuffed Tomatoes, 141
Summer Trifle, 200
Surprise Potatoes, 139
Swedes Cooked to Perfection, 120
Sweet and Sour Cabbage, 178
Sweet Corn Bake, 127
Sweet Creamy Sauce, 205
Tea Ring, 222
Thick Cheese Sauce, 190
Tomato Jelly Salad, 103
Tomato Ketchup, 239
Tomato Sauce, 238
Tomato Soup, 91

Tossed Carrots, 111
Tossed Green Salad, 94
Tripe in Cider, 171

Vegetable Casserole, 142
Vegetable Curry, 180
Vegetable Stock, 236
Vegetarian 'Gravy', 146
Venison Casserole, 168

Watercress Soup, 92
Welsh Barley Bread, 229
Wheat Pudding, *see* Frumenty
Wholemeal Bread, 219
Wholemeal Shortcrust Pastry, 210

Yogurt, 244
Yogurt Salad Dressing, 108

Two more books by Patrick Rivers

LIVING BETTER ON LESS

A timely and stimulating book for all those who, by choice or circumstances, are having to tighten their belts because of the ravages of inflation, the fall in real incomes, or the stark reality of redundancy.

Here is a real alternative to the rat race, through which you can rediscover what you *really* need. Living on less is not only possible, but desirable – for the planet, for other people, and for your own inner and outer well-being.

LIVING BETTER ON LESS is packed with exciting possibilities and hard facts. By adopting only a fraction of its advice and practical ideas you can save the cost of the book *every week* for the rest of your life.

LIVING ON A LITTLE LAND

Having been made redundant, Patrick Rivers left city life to return to the land. With his wife Shirley he bought eight steep, derelict and rubbish-strewn acres with a ruined cottage. Now the land carries goats, sheep, poultry, bees, fruit and vegetables, and the cottage has been restored.

This book tells the story of that transformation, detailing the mistakes as well as the successes for those who, like Patrick and Shirley Rivers, take on a firm commitment to live simply and literally within their means.

LIVING ON A LITTLE LAND offers practical guidance, asks many basic questions about the oft-vaunted ideal of self-sufficiency, and, in a fascinating story, gives one family's answers.

Both books available from:
**TURNSTONE PRESS LIMITED
Wellingborough, Northamptonshire**